MINING THE CA$H HIDDEN IN YOUR BUSINESS

Increase Cash Flow
and Decrease Financing Requirements
by Reducing Working Capital

Wayne H. Smith

Published by Working Capital Concepts LLC, Santa Barbara, CA

ISBN 978-0-9857554-0-9

Library of Congress Control Number: 2012948641

Printed in the USA

First Edition, September 2012

www.workingcapitalconcepts.com

Dear Kamran, 11/15/2012

Thank you for your interest in my book. Also thanks for the endorsement on LinkedIn. Any comments you may have would be appreciated. Best regards Hayne

I dedicate this book to my wife, Barbara,
without whose support, encouragement and understanding
I would not have been able to write it.

Her editing was above and beyond the call of duty.
For this I shall ever be grateful.

CONTENTS

PREFACE

This book's time has come. *Mining The Ca$h Hidden in Your Business* is an audacious title but bank credit is very tight, the economy is slow and businesses are struggling to find capital to grow. Over the years I have tried to find a book to help operating managers understand how to drive down working capital and increase cash flow so they could finance their businesses with internally generated funds. I have never found one on this subject. Thus, the idea to write a book giving a holistic view of working capital management evolved. This book provides practical methods to manage working capital and improve cash flow. There are numerous redundant phrases and passages in this book. This is by design. I want to drive home the importance of the primary concepts so they become part of your business vocabulary.

My initial awareness that working capital management played an important role in the success of a company came in a finance class during my second year at The Harvard Business School. My class was assigned a case study concerning a growing and profitable company that had to close its doors because it could not pay its suppliers. My classmates and I analyzed and debated the case without reaching a conclusion as to why the company had failed. At one point in the discussion the professor said we had all missed the fact that the company could not finance the increase in inventory and accounts receivable resulting from the sales growth. The company did not have sufficient internally generated funds and the bank would not increase the company's credit line so it could pay its suppliers. The company had to liquidate to meet payment demands. This was a huge eye-opener for me on the importance of minimizing working capital.

I spent a major part of my business career developing programs to increase cash flow and reduce financing requirements by reducing working capital. The value chain analysis concept was developed early in my business life while trying to find better ways to reduce accounts receivable in the foreign operations of a large multinational food company.

In my first major business assignment, I was the credit manager for a large chemical company's Latin American operations. Customers were using the company as a bank. Days of sales in accounts receivable was 180 and there were bankruptcies throughout the region. What an initiation for me into the world of credit management! That early experience convinced me that receivables management issues were much larger than the scope of the finance department and needed general management attention. Later on, as I worked at other manufacturing companies, I came to realize that driving down working capital is a strategic business issue. The concepts I discuss in this book evolved over time as I strove to reduce working capital. I observed that highly successful businesses adopting the philosophy of less working capital actually improved customer service.

The processes discussed in this book have been used successfully to reduce working capital. Installing effective working capital reduction programs results in improved cash flow, energized employees and happy customers, suppliers and investors.

This book presents a straightforward, no-nonsense discussion of the steps to take to drive down working capital to zero or lower. The ideas are action-oriented. The book is operationally oriented and not meant to be a major thesis on finance.

ACKNOWLEDGEMENTS

During my business career, I have had the pleasure of being associated with a number of talented professionals. Gaining knowledge was cumulative, starting with The University of Michigan School of Engineering and Harvard Business School. The U.S. Navy also played a strong role in my development as a leader. Many people at The Dow Chemical Company, The Quaker Oats Company and Avery Dennison Corporation helped me develop my business skill set.

During my time at Quaker Oats, I had the privilege of working with Peter Fritsche and Dick Jaquith. Peter was a no-nonsense M&A guy and very competitive. He taught me how to analyze an acquisition candidate from stem to stern, with a focus particularly on working capital. He was a bulldog who never gave up trying to find a better answer. Dick, a very smart finance person, showed extreme patience in teaching me treasury management, particularly international finance with an emphasis on foreign exchange exposure management.

Phil Neal and Greg Jenkins were my mentors at Avery Dennison. Phil tested me with a "So what?" question on every slide I showed him. Greg pushed me to get all my thoughts on an issue on one page. Watching Geoff Martin and his team at Avery turn antiquated plants into gleaming modern manufacturing facilities was an inspiration.

There are several people who helped me develop this book with ideas and encouragement. I want to thank Bill Wayne and Eric Ball for reading the material and giving me valuable comments. Dave Schmidt provided some truly thoughtful ideas.

Finally, this book was a family affair. My wife Barbara painstakingly edited the material and our daughter Emily provided critical input on marketing and organization. Our daughter Liz gave me tremendous insight on liability exposure and risk management.

Chapter 1

INTRODUCTION

Reducing working capital will increase cash flow and reduce financing requirements

Driving down working capital can significantly increase cash flow and improve financial results. You can reduce the amount of financing required to grow a business by reducing working capital and increasing cash flow. In a recent study that I conducted of fifteen U.S. manufacturing companies, operating working capital as a percentage of sales averaged 22.5%. This finding is consistent with a major study of the operating working capital of many U.S. manufacturing companies. Furthermore, operating working capital as a percentage of total invested capital, net of excess cash, averaged about 29%. It is clear from this data that reducing working capital can have a significant impact on the level of invested capital and increase cash flow in a business. You should be able to significantly reduce working capital by following the techniques described in this book. Excessive inventory and slow-paying customers are two of the biggest challenges for businesses, both large and small. Collecting from slow-paying customers is particularly difficult. This book lists the actions to take to reduce receivables and make sure you have the correct inventory to meet customer demand.

My experience reducing working capitol

This book is the culmination of a wealth of professional experience. During my tenure as Vice President and Treasurer of a Fortune 500 company it embarked on a program to reduce working capital. The objective was to increase cash flow and reduce invested capital, thus increasing the return on total capital (ROTC). Over a period of years operating working capital declined 30%, from 19.6% to 13.7% of sales. This resulted in a $230 million reduction in capital required to operate the business. At the same time, ROTC increased from 7.1% to 19.7% with part of the improvement due to lower invested capital.

Most of the improvement in working capital resulted from an increase in inventory turnover. There was also an increase in accounts payable. Improvements in cash management had already been done. The company had significant success in reducing accounts receivable in its major European division. This improvement was offset by a rapid growth of accounts receivable in Asia. Without the reduction in days of sales outstanding in accounts receivable (DSO) in Europe, the company would not have achieved such a sharp decline in overall levels of working capital.

Operating working capital as a percentage of sales today is down to 13.2%, even with operating cash of 3% of sales up from 0.3% due to cash trapped overseas. Maintaining a low level of operating working capital has helped the company remain profitable during a particularly difficult worldwide economic period.

Running a business with minimal operating working capital

You can manage a business with almost no operating working capital. This means you are financing current assets primarily with non-interest-bearing current liabilities. A company that adopts the philosophy of operating with minimal working capital will have to undergo some changes in its business practices and processes. However, your customers will appreciate the improved service and your shareholders will be very pleased when they see the increased cash flow resulting from lower costs and lower investment. In addition, you should have increased sales growth as your customers buy more products resulting from better service and product quality. These improved results will drive significant increases in shareholder value. Finally, and perhaps most importantly, your employees will be more motivated due to a better work environment.

Seven fundamental strategies to reduce working capital

The following concepts are fundamental to minimizing working capital. They must be ingrained in your team's thinking. Doing so will change the culture of the company to one of minimizing working capital and maximizing customer service. These concepts are simple and easy to remember. All employees will begin to think of them as the operating philosophy of the company. It is important to articulate the concepts in actionable ideas. You must educate your employees on a new way of running the business. Having easy-to-remember phrases that describe what you are trying to accomplish will make it simpler to change the business practices and procedures.

The seven concepts are as follows:

- Take time, defects, non-value-added work and variation out of all processes.
- Maintain zero operating cash but have credit lines available to manage cash flow variation and strategic cash reserves for major identified risks and investment opportunities.
- Manufacture and ship what you sell as expediently as possible.
- Make it easy for your customers to pay quickly.
- Have key materials delivered frequently to meet production requirements.
- Pay supplier invoices only when payment is expected.
- Require all stakeholders to have a financial investment in the business.

This is a very simplistic view of business management. However, many small businesses operate in this manner. People with no capital operate this way out of necessity. You can manage a highly successful, large and growing business in the same manner.

Advantages of a minimal working capital strategy

A strategy of minimizing operating working capital has a number of advantages for a company. The most important benefit is improved customer service through faster, more reliable delivery of zero-defect products and services. Having a very low level of working capital creates a culture of:

- Intense customer focus and customer service
- No tolerance of defects in processes and products
- Continuous improvement
- Increasing economic value through reduced costs and reduced investment
- A sustainable competitive advantage through outstanding product quality, excellent customer service and a very low cost and investment structure

One more big benefit is that your employees will be fully involved in the process and they will be highly motivated by the program. They will own it. You will have to turn many activities over to them that were previously done in an office behind a closed door. That won't work anymore. This is participative capitalism. The shop floor runs the plant. A highly paid consultant once said, "Every employee walks thought the door every day with a brain for free. Use it!" Utilizing your employees' capabilities to the maximum is what this program is all about.

Operating working capital definition

My definition of operating working capital is current assets, excluding strategic cash and current deferred taxes receivable, less current liabilities, excluding short-term debt, other accrued liabilities, current taxes payable and current deferred taxes payable. This is the capital used to operate a business on a day-to-day basis. Capital needed to finance the investment in accounts receivable and inventory can be financed with non-interest-bearing liabilities such as accounts payable and accrued payroll and employee benefits. The accounting profession includes short-term debt in the definition of working capital because current liabilities include all obligations with a maturity of less than one year.

Managing working capital is separate from how it is financed

The financing of working capital is, in general, irrelevant to how it is managed. The amount of short-term and long-term debt is a function of the company's earning power, cash flow and the availability and cost of various types of financing. The financing strategy for working capital should take into account the amount of working capital, but that is only one of many considerations in deciding how to finance the business.

The financing strategy of the business depends on the long-term cash flow forecast and the current and projected capital structure of the company. It also depends on the market position of the company in its industry and the strength of its competitors, the volatility of the industry, and the size of the company and markets served. The size of the company and years in business play an important role in determining financing strategy. In the cash management chapter, I will discuss using short-term debt to manage cash flow, thus avoiding excess operating cash. I will also discuss how to determine the maximum and minimum amount of short-term debt required to manage cash flow.

Working capital minimization is a strategic initiative

A working capital minimization program is a strategic initiative. It is a key business issue that touches all parts of the enterprise. It is not a finance problem that is to be left to the chief financial officer (CFO) to manage. Likewise, it is not strictly a supply chain issue. The Chief Operating Officer (COO) or Chief Executive Officer (CEO) are probably the best candidates to run the program. The person in charge has to see the process as one that adds value to customers all along the value chain from acquiring an order to putting cash in the bank. If reducing working capital ends up being a cost reduction program or an extension of supply chain management, it will probably fail and simply become the corporate program of the week.

Significantly reducing working capital requires operational excellence

Minimizing working capital requires you to have operational excellence. It is about achieving and maintaining outstanding execution of robust business practices. Operational excellence is a critical part of any business strategy. Installing the procedures outlined in this book is hard work. It takes courage to implement some of the actions to achieve the desired results. In some of the businesses I have observed, true visionaries were at work installing radical practices to drive down working capital. The new ideas were very successful and the companies thrived. You don't have to be a revolutionary to significantly reduce working capital. However, you do have to want to make changes in the way you do business.

Your employees must manage the program

In the following pages I will show you how to start on the path toward reducing working capital. This is a long-term project requiring the effort of employees from all parts of the company. Use your own people to do the work. After all, they run the business. Give them ample training to transition to the new approach of managing the day-to-day operations of the company. Make sure your people are deeply involved in the project from analysis through design and implementation. You should not make major changes in your fundamental business practices without first reviewing the proposed changes with either customers or suppliers if they are impacted by the changes.

Your employees will also be a valuable source of ideas to improve process effectiveness. They know the company. To make your manufacturing and administrative processes error-free you will have to take time, defects, non-value-added work and variation out of the activities in these areas. Your employees will know where to look for problems and have many suggestions for improvement. To do this you will also have to measure and analyze everything from delivery reliability from the customer's perspective to various aspects of product quality. Measure everything that is critical in delivering a defect-free product to the customer on time and for collecting quickly. Involve your employees at every step of the program.

Reducing working capital does not require a major systems upgrade

Significantly reducing working capital usually does not require a major computer systems upgrade. Most of the concepts in this book are straightforward, easy to apply strategies that use your existing systems in a more robust manner. Inventory management and related supply chain management systems may require specialized programs that can be purchased off the shelf and integrated with existing systems. You may need some assistance to install and set up a demand-forecasting program.

Employee productivity will increase

Increasing production speed and flexibility will reduce manufacturing cycle time. This can be accomplished by reducing production defects, decreasing production line set-up time and increasing line speed. These actions will require the concerted effort of your team but the payoff is an increase in employee productivity. In many cases, fixing production issues will drive down working capital. With fewer defects and increased production speed and flexibility you will be able to quickly ship a very high-quality product. This should result in lower inventory, faster collection and lower unit labor costs.

Finding a factory within a factory

Once you have reduced product defects and manufacturing cycle time you will need less inventory, free up productive capacity and lower costs. This equates to an expansion of your factory and warehouse at no cost. It is like finding a factory within a factory. In addition to having a lower labor cost per unit, you will reduce all your other manufacturing costs, including scrap and energy. You will be able to collect accounts receivable faster due to fewer defective product claims and invoicing errors. This will lead to significantly lower costs, a lower total investment base and increased cash flow, giving you a significant sustainable competitive advantage.

Focus on key customers and suppliers

A central part of the program is to focus on the key customers and suppliers who generate 80% to 90% of the transaction flow. Learn how to work more efficiently with them from ordering through collection. These top customers and suppliers generate most of the activity in your company. Carefully understanding your top twenty customers and suppliers will provide insight on how to take time and cost out of your processes. Share demand data with customers and suppliers. This will require trust from all parties involved.

Benchmark financial performance

Another part of getting started is to benchmark your financial performance including, but not limited to, operating margin, return on total capital, working capital as a percentage of sales, inventory turnover, DSO (days of sales outstanding in accounts receivable), and DPO (days of payables outstanding) against your competitors, customers and suppliers. This will give you a good reference point from the beginning to measure your performance over time relative to others. Using this analysis will definitely give you a perspective on what is acceptable and the norm in your industry. However, this is just a starting point. Be careful about accepting industry norms. Vision and tenacity are needed to drive out inefficiency in your business.

Focus on reducing working capital

As discussed in the first part of this chapter, reducing working capital can significantly improve cash flow and reduce invested capital. It is important to focus on working capital for a number of other reasons. By definition, working capital is an investment that is liquid and recoverable within one year. However, working capital is a permanent investment in the business. Once you start manufacturing and selling a product you will have accounts receivable and inventory for as long as you are operating. The investment in accounts receivable and inventory is financed by a non-financial investor only to the extent that you owe someone for goods or services. Assuming your business is a going concern, you will always have a need for working capital unless you can make current assets equal to non-financial current liabilities. Working capital will only decline if sales decline or through better working capital management. Better working capital management is clearly preferred over a decline in sales.

If you have twenty cents of every dollar of sales invested in working capital, then you have to invest twenty cents for every dollar of incremental sales. That may not sound like much but if you are going to grow sales $1,000,000 next year you will need 20% of the increase or $200,000 to fund working capital. This is exclusive of any capital equipment investment. Unless your have excess cash in the bank you will have to obtain external financing. If you have no working capital or even 5% of sales invested in working capital, your ability to finance growth with internally generated funds will be much more manageable. As stated earlier, in my study of manufacturing companies, the average operating working capital was 22.5% of sales and about 29% of invested capital. Reducing operating working capital will have a major impact on cash flow, the level of invested capital and financing requirements.

Having low working capital is also important in helping a company gain a competitive advantage. A lower investment base provides more latitude in running the business. For example, the company can be more aggressive on pricing or it can increase spending on R&D or marketing. This is a significant advantage relative to competitors.

Even if sales decline, working capital won't decline proportionally unless you are managing working capital very closely. The main reason is because accounts receivable usually do not get collected on time. Customers become very creative with a myriad of excuses not to pay an invoice when business conditions tighten. This often results in having the wrong inventory on hand to fill new orders. You then have a chronic slow-moving inventory problem and inventory begins to increase. The accounts receivable clerk at your supplier doesn't care that the material you ordered is not required and you have a cash flow problem. Your supplier wants to be paid on time for material delivered.

Focus on taking time and errors out of processes

Near zero operating working capital can be achieved by minimizing current assets and maximizing non-interest-bearing current liabilities. The focus is on taking time and errors out of processes to minimize the investment in current assets. You cannot win the war by not paying suppliers on time. That game just won't work in the long term. In the end being a chronic late payer results in negative actions by suppliers such as being placed on credit hold when a critical part is needed or being placed in allocation when a part has a limited supply. However, you do need to negotiate very competitive pricing and credit terms from all suppliers while assuring fast delivery and zero defects.

Programs that have long-term benefits include developing just-in-time delivery programs for customers and just-in-time inventory management programs with suppliers, automating collection and payment systems, minimizing set-up time in production, minimizing product line complexity, minimizing supplier complexity, installing cellular manufacturing, achieving a zero recordable injury rate, and much more. The key is to take time, variation, non-value-added work and defects out of all processes. This will dramatically increase production flexibility, speed and reliability. You will see this mentioned many times in the following pages.

Some companies have adopted Lean Six Sigma as the approach to take in reducing working capital. Other companies have utilized a variety of quality improvement programs. Do what works best and is affordable for your company as long as you move toward increased production speed, fewer product and administrative defects and increased production flexibility.

Historically, high levels of working capital viewed as important

It is important to take a brief look at the historical concept of working capital. Many credit analysts look at working capital as a measure of financial liquidity. That is correct if the company has no working capital because it has no positive cash flow. Financial analysts put great emphasis on the current ratio (current assets divided by current liabilities) and the quick ratio (accounts receivable and cash divided by current liabilities.) These ratios have to be greater than one, and, in the case of the current ratio, should be two to one for the company to be considered financially strong. These measures ignore cash flow and the earning power (operating margins, return on investment and value creation ability) of the company. We know today that the ability to generate free cash flow is the true measure of the liquidity of a company. The less working capital that is required to operate the business, the greater the cash flow. Credit rating agencies now focus on cash flow from operations to total debt and earnings before interest and taxes to fixed charges. The larger the cash flow from operations relative to sales and debt, the higher the credit rating, making it easier to finance growth with debt.

Techniques can be used in non-manufacturing

Most of the discussion in this book references manufacturing companies. However, these techniques can be used in financial and service industries. I know of a data processing outsourcing service provider that used these techniques to reduce working capital. The company determined that it should have credit terms equal to its service life cycle, in this case one to two weeks down from 30 days, with payment made by direct debit rather than check. It also required employees to be paid two weeks after they performed their service with a one-week processing time. The company also renegotiated the credit terms on the computer lease contract from 30 to 60 days. Accounts receivable, lease accounts payable and accrued payroll were the three largest working capital items. By shortening the receivables cycle, lengthening lease payment terms and lengthening the payroll cycle, the company moved to slightly negative working capital. The company then was in a position to grow without incremental outside investment. This was very good for the employees since they now worked for a growing company. The company even used this approach to buy out a competitor. The new approach to working capital management changed the company's business model. It learned to carefully manage working capital after very painfully going through several years of near bankruptcy. With the new approach it created a profitable, growing business generating positive cash flow.

Summary

The entire working capital reduction process is very circular. Improving one part of working capital will help improve another area. All components of working capital will have obvious quick-hit improvements that can be made early in the program, resulting in big benefits. This can come from improving the order entry procedures to reduce errors. It can also come from changing ordering and delivery of high consumption items from monthly to weekly or even daily. Once the organization and structure is designed, the progress of reducing working capital will come from understanding the details of the processes and making them fast, flexible and error-free.

The working capital minimization concept is applicable in many different industries in countries around the globe. No one should be exempt from striving to minimize working capital to zero or lower by saying his/her company is different from others. You can eliminate working capital. The key is to start now with a well-designed program.

This book is divided into two main sections: *Getting Started* and *Taking Action*. In *Getting Started*, some definitions, organization considerations, process analysis and performance measurement will be reviewed. The fun begins with *Taking Action*. Good preparation before you take action is critical. This is a step-by-step approach to establishing programs that achieve a large reduction in working capital, thereby significantly improving cash flow. You can do the work with your organization. However, before making any significant changes you should review the proposed actions with your outside auditors, lawyers, and commercial bankers. They can give you an external perspective on the accounting, legal and financial impact of what you are about to implement.

Chapter 2

GETTING STARTED

Before taking direct action on the individual components of working capital you need to do some preparatory work. Obviously, as soon as you identify a big impact quick-fix project you should take the time to make the improvement. However, once the project is finished you should complete the basic framework for attacking working capital reduction in a systematic manner.

The actions to accomplish before beginning to improve the specific components of working capital are:

- Establish an organization structure
- Define working capital
- Analyze financial and working capital performance for the last twenty quarters
- Design and install financial performance measures
- Analyze the value chain

Once you have completed these steps you are ready to begin taking action on the individual components of working capital to drive it to zero or lower. These first five steps will lay a foundation for achieving significant working capital reduction. You will have an organization and structure in place that will allow you to manage the reduction process in an orderly manner. You will also have a baseline against which you can measure progress.

Each of these five steps will be fully discussed in the following chapters. Before going straight to them, I will give you an overview of what you will be covering.

Organization

You must have a senior management level steering committee that meets periodically to review strategy and performance against targets and determine next steps. Each steering committee representative should be responsible for a part of the working capital reduction program. All steering committee members should have some of their bonus dependent on achieving specific working capital targets.

Working capital definition

Defining what you mean by the term working capital is extremely important. Make sure everyone in the company understands what you are doing and what working capital means. This step accomplishes the buy-in of the program from the organization.

Analyze past performance

Analyzing past financial and working capital performance is necessary to establish a baseline against which you can measure progress in driving down working capital. Develop a core group of similar companies against which you can compare your performance.

Performance measures

Designing and installing performance measures that are linked to compensation plans is critical to the success of the working capital reduction program. If you don't measure what you want to manage, no improvement will take place. These measures need to be linked to bonus compensation programs. The monthly and quarterly reports of actual performance against targets need to be prominently displayed for all employees to view. Hold employee meetings to discuss progress and next steps. Communication is extremely important.

Analyze the value chain

Analyzing the value chain is the key to determining where you can take time, defects, non-value-added work and variation out of the revenue and cost cycles. This activity will touch every process and area of your company. It is important to do this work very carefully.

If you follow these five steps properly you should find some large working capital reduction opportunities that you can go after immediately. Analyzing past performance should point out areas for improvement, particularly if you compare your company against a group of similar companies.

Almost all of what is advocated in this book can be achieved with existing systems and technology. New ERP systems are not necessary to accomplish what is recommended. The assumption is that you have installed a relatively robust computer system to do the basic accounting. If that is true, you can move forward. In many cases existing computer systems are underutilized and have much more available power than is currently being used.

While these steps may seem rather rudimentary and obvious, they are critical to the success of the program. Most companies do not have a well-structured and cohesive working capital reduction program. They overlook many factors that go into driving down working capital to zero or below. I am recommending a very straightforward, simple approach to systematically analyze each component of working capital and determine how to optimize its level for a particular company's business circumstances.

Chapter 3

ORGANIZATION

A solid organizational structure is required to systematically reduce working capital in your company. You cannot significantly reduce working capital unless you have installed a very robust organization and program. The steps to take in developing a powerful structure are as follows:

- Select a committed leader.
- Appoint a strong steering committee team.
- Select individual teams for each working capital component.
- Establish a workspace to hold information and personnel, if any, working full time on the project.
- Develop an employee communication program.
- Establish a training program.

Select a committed leader

The leader must be visionary. Select a committed person to run the team overseeing the working capital reduction program. The leader must have the authority and power to implement the changes needed to take time, defects, non-value-added work and variation out of the order-to-cash cycle. In most companies, this will either be the CEO or COO. It is preferable that the chairperson of the steering committee be a very senior operating person. The CFO must be a team member but if the CFO heads the project it may be viewed as a finance project. That is not the message you want to send to the organization.

Driving down working capital is a strategic business issue. A leading management consultant states many times in his lectures that a company cannot grow unless it has its working capital under control and has programs in place to reduce working capital. Working capital reduction and the elimination of product and process defects are the cornerstones of a growth strategy.

Individual team members

The CFO should be responsible for installing and reporting on the performance measures. The CFO should also be responsible for taking action against all working capital components other than accounts receivable, inventory and accounts payable. These three components of working capital are very operational and need the full attention of the sales, marketing, manufacturing, materials management, logistics and purchasing operations. The leaders of each component should be on the steering committee that oversees the working capital reduction program. These are the key people required to make decisions to drive fundamental changes in the way the business is managed day-to-day. They must have outstanding execution skills. This is not a strategic planning exercise. You want action-oriented change agents managing the process to accomplish a major change in the way you operate the business.

The first meeting of the leadership steering committee team should focus on selecting the working capital definition and performance measures. This may sound like a finance job. However, it is extremely important that each member of the team be involved in shaping these basic definitions and measures to achieve buy-in. I have witnessed large debates on day's sales outstanding in accounts receivable and return on investment calculations simply because the operating units being measured did not understand the background behind the calculation process nor were they involved in the initial discussions when the definitions were developed.

Select individual team members for each component of working capital

The members required for each major working capital reduction team will be reviewed throughout the book. It is important to select team members who are change agents.

Form four teams in addition to the steering committee. These are:

- Accounts receivable
- Inventory
- Accounts payable
- Other current assets and liabilities

Members of the finance function must be fully responsible for the other current assets and liabilities action programs as follows:

- Cash minimization
- Other current assets minimization
- Accrued payroll and employee benefits maximization

Separate teams should be established for each of these activities.

You will need input from human resources and legal advice in any payroll payment changes. It is also necessary to review all these accounts with appropriate operating personnel. Most of the balances in these accounts will result from operating decisions and they must be carefully reviewed.

Establish a work space

Having a separate workspace is critical. Some companies call it a war room, which may sound melodramatic. However, having a separate space sets the tone for the program. Select a location to hold meetings and staff, if any. Post results from the various teams in this location. The space allocation makes a statement that this is serious business and resources are being devoted to the project. The Ford Motor Company has used this technique very successfully in its turnaround program.

Communicate the program to employees

Communication is a key factor. Hold informational meetings and produce written communications for employees. Public display of the project's results against targets in graphical form will be very important. Someone needs to be in charge of project communications if it is to succeed.

Establish a training program

Training will be a major effort in your working capital reduction program and requires someone to take on this responsibility. In bigger companies, representatives from the human resources department should be on the committee and take responsibility for training. Training is the key to changing the way employees think and act as they perform their daily tasks. People will be asked to make decisions that previously were made by someone else. For example, the team running a manufacturing cell will be responsible for reordering raw materials and packaging supplies and scheduling production and preventative maintenance. These new skills have to be learned. The tasks need to be discussed and understood before being implemented.

Some employees will not want to change. If so, you may have to replace some of the workforce. This can be difficult and time-consuming. However, without a committed workforce, you will not be able to significantly lower working capital.

Chapter 4

WORKING CAPITAL DEFINITION

Develop a comprehensive definition and obtain buy-in

Once the team is formed, develop a comprehensive definition of working capital that is accepted by each member. Buy-in of the definition by the team is critical to the success of the project. Team members are more likely to accept the project if they are included in defining the performance measures.

Definition focuses on operating working capital

My working capital definition is based on an operating working capital approach. I include all current assets except strategic excess cash and current deferred taxes receivable and all current liabilities except short-term debt, other accrued liabilities and current taxes payable and current deferred taxes payable. This definition is easy to compute from the accounting records and includes the key operating components of working capital. The strategic cash and short-term debt exclusion needs to be fully discussed in the definition phase. I will expand on strategic excess cash and short-term debt in the chapter on cash management. The main point is that the definition of working capital I use focuses on total operating working capital. All of the accounts included can be managed and controlled by the operating management of the company.

Include all operational current assets and liabilities

Accounts receivable, inventory and accounts payable are sometimes the only accounts included in the definition of operating working capital. These three accounts are where you will want to put the majority of your effort. However, do not ignore the other smaller components of working capital including operating cash, other receivables, prepaid expenses, and accrued payroll and employee benefits. These accounts can have a major influence on working capital and can be impacted by management action to either minimize or maximize the balances as may be appropriate. The smaller components of current assets can be as much as 2% to 5% of sales. Cutting this level of investment in half is a meaningful reduction in working capital. I have seen this magnitude of reduction. Someone must be accountable for the balances in all the working capital accounts and be able to explain the reason for the amounts in each account. If you don't include the smaller components of working capital you will miss a significant opportunity to reduce the operating working capital required to run the business.

Include only operating cash

I only include operating cash in my definition of working capital. In the study I conducted, the lowest level of cash was 2% of sales. This equates to about one week of sales. This is the minimum level of operating cash for most companies. In the study, total cash and investments averaged 15.6% of sales and ranged from 2% to 50% of sales. Unfortunately, most companies mix operating and strategic cash. They don't really manage them separately nor do they even think of them as separate accounts. These companies feel cash is cash and the total pool can be managed together. There are really two pools of cash in almost every company and they need to be managed separately. Exclude from your definition of working capital all cash items and marketable securities that are held to satisfy a strategic objective. This strategic cash balance should be managed to meet the strategic objective. Operating cash should be managed to meet the operating needs of the business. Cash balances held for longer-term needs can be invested with a longer maturity, thus generating increased investment income. Cash held to satisfy very short-term requirements must be invested in liquid instruments that will usually have a low yield.

Exclude short-term debt

Exclude all short-term debt from the working capital definition. The financing of working capital has no bearing on how it is managed. However, it is important to structure total debt to have part of it short-term so it will be available to be repaid with any positive cash flow. The overall financing strategy will determine the total short-term debt level.

Detailed definition

Current operating assets less current non-interest-bearing liabilities equal total operating working capital. The accounts included in my definition of operating working capital are as follows:

Cash (operating)
Accounts receivable (net of reserves for bad debts and returns and allowances)
Inventory (net of reserves)
Other current assets (other receivables and prepaid expenses)
    Current operating assets

Less:
Trade payables
Accrued payroll and employee benefits
    Current operating liabilities

Once you have agreed on a working capital definition with the leadership team you should perform an analysis of working capital over the last twenty quarters.

You can do this as part of the performance measurement analysis discussed in the next chapter. Analyze each component of working capital as a percentage of annualized quarterly sales. This must be done in addition to computing days of sales outstanding in accounts receivables (DSO), inventory turnover and days of payables outstanding (DPO) for each of the quarters.

Some obvious issues may be apparent

Some conclusions will be apparent based on the trends and absolute levels of the components. For example, if DSO is 55 and DPO is 25, your payables terms may be significantly shorter than your credit terms or customer willingness to pay. The imbalance needs to be addressed either by reducing DSO through shorter credit terms or lengthening DPO through longer supplier terms or a combination of the two actions. Also, if inventory turnover is three times a year and your product has a manufacturing cycle of one week, you may be holding too much inventory.

Analysis provides a benchmark

Analyzing performance may seem like a trivial exercise to engage in at the beginning of the project when everyone on the team wants to jump in and take action. You must do the performance measurement and working capital analysis along with the value chain analysis to have a benchmark from which to measure progress. It will also be very helpful in identifying obvious areas that need attention. Your organization cannot go in too many directions at once. One large, focused project could have multiple benefits. For example, to attack a very low inventory turnover situation you need to focus on operational excellence in manufacturing to improve product quality and production flexibility. Improving manufacturing effectiveness and driving down inventory will also improve collections. With fewer product quality issues and better delivery reliability, there will be fewer reasons for your customers to not pay on time.

Chapter 5

PERFORMANCE MEASUREMENT

Performance measurement is a central part of the program

Understanding and properly using performance measures is a central part of making a working capital minimization program successful. Some of the information in this chapter is not intuitively obvious. You might even disagree with a few of the performance measures and definitions. However, you must have basic performance measures tied to compensation for the working capital reduction program to be truly effective. *What's measured gets managed.* This may be a cliché but it is true.

Link performance measurement and compensation

Link the achievement of performance measurement targets with compensation. If you pay bonuses for meeting the measured targets, the result will be improved performance. Provide a monetary incentive for your people to achieve certain written, quantifiable objectives. If you don't have written annual objectives you should stop here and work on your compensation and human resources management programs before trying to do anything with the concepts in this book. Operating cash flow should be a key measure for bonus purposes along with net income and sales growth.

Start measuring at the beginning of the program

If you don't measure it you can't fix it. This is the corollary to the *what gets measured gets managed* statement. Begin by measuring operating working capital as a percentage of sales. Start talking about it and reporting on it.

Make the components of working capital part of the culture. Days of sales outstanding in accounts receivable (DSO), inventory turnover and days of accounts payables outstanding (DPO) must be understood and a part of the company's vocabulary.

Appendix A is an example of the financial analysis you should perform at the beginning of the program. The example demonstrates how to perform the calculations for working capital and financial performance measures. Install them in your business. Begin by analyzing the measures over the last twenty quarters. This analysis will give you a good overview of the financial trends in your business.

DEFINITIONS FOR OPERATING WORKING CAPITAL MEASURES

Operating working capital as a percentage of sales

This is current assets, excluding strategic cash and current deferred taxes receivable less non-interest-bearing current liabilities excluding short-term debt, other accrued liabilities, current taxes payable and current deferred taxes payable divided by sales times 100%. Make this calculation at least quarterly using annualized quarterly sales. A monthly calculation is desirable. You can use a trailing annualized three-month sales base for the monthly calculation. Also compute each component of operating working capital as a percentage of sales.

Day's sales outstanding in accounts receivable (DSO)

This is accounts receivable, net of reserves, divided by average daily sales for the period. The time period should be the approximate time to collect accounts receivable. Calculate this number each month using trailing three-month sales for the sales base. Changes in reserves can influence DSO in the short term but over time these changes will not matter. Calculate DSO gross and net of reserves and DSO by each aging category. Current DSO should approximate your weighted average credit terms.

Inventory turnover

This is cost of goods sold divided by inventory. It should be calculated quarterly using annualized quarterly cost of goods sold. The inventory should be net of reserves. If possible you should calculate this monthly using the most recent quarterly income statement annualized cost of goods sold.

Day's payable outstanding (DPO)

This is accounts payable divided by average daily cost of goods sold. The average daily cost of goods sold should be calculated over a time period approximating supplier terms. Calculate this monthly to the extent possible. You can use the average daily cost of goods sold for the previous quarter to simplify the calculation if you don't prepare a monthly income statement. This is a measure of credit terms extended by suppliers.

These four measures cover the main components of working capital. Each group managing these functions and other aspects of working capital will utilize additional measures but the focus needs to be on the four measures as defined in this section.

Measures should be trended over time

All of these measures are somewhat crude and should be trended over time. The important thing is to analyze the trend. All of these ratios and measures should be debated and agreed upon by the steering committee at the beginning of the program. Focus on the results rather than the calculation methodology and get behind the numbers. If you are shipping to customers in 48 hours of receipt of the order and the product is used immediately in their manufacturing process, why do you need to give the customer 30-day terms? Do you really need three months of cost of sales in inventory? Why can't it be one month or two weeks? Look at the ratios and begin to ask honest questions about why they are so high or, in the case of payables, so low.

Key financial measures

Financial measures are important in helping to understand performance and guide decision-making. Focus on these key financial measures:

- **Sales** are the revenue of the company. Sale growth should also be measured. Sales and sales growth are your first priority with cash flow a close second.

- **Gross margin** is gross profit divided by sales and is a key measure of earning power.

- **Earnings before interest and taxes (EBIT)** are a key measure of profitability. Some analysts define EBIT as operating income. However, many companies include interest expense in computing operating income. Some analysts focus on earnings before interest, taxes, depreciation and amortization (EBITDA). That is more of a measure of cash flow before taxes. It is probably a good short-term measure of ability to pay but if you don't recover your full costs of operation over time you will not survive. Therefore, focus on EBIT.

- **Operating margin** is EBIT divided by sales. The trend of operating margin over time is a very important indicator of the health of the company.

- **Net income** is the income of the company after all expenses including taxes.

- **Return on sales (ROS)** is net income divided by sales.

- **Interest coverage** is EBIT divided by interest expense.

- **Operating cash flow** is net income plus non-cash charges less changes in operating working capital and capital expenditures.

- **Operating cash flow as a % of sales** measures a company's ability to generate cash.

- **Total debt to total capital** is total debt (short-term debt plus long-term debt) divided by total debt plus equity.

- **Return on equity (ROE)** is net income divided by shareholders' equity. Some analysts calculate ROE using average equity for the period.

- **Return on total capital (ROTC)** is net income plus after-tax interest expense divided by total capital employed in the business. Total capital is all debt, including short-term debt, plus equity. Some analysts make the calculation using average total capital for the period. This measure eliminates the impact of financing. It includes taxes, which can substantially impact return on investment. You can impact returns by locating a business in a low tax area. Operating management needs to understand the impact of taxes. For example, Hong Kong has an 16.5% tax rate compared with Japan at 38%. All other things being equal, returns on capital will be higher in Hong Kong than Japan.

- **Total debt to operating cash flow** is the measure of how quickly debt can be repaid.

In some businesses and industries, economic value added is used to determine how well a company is creating economic value. It can be used to examine the economic impact of business decisions. Economic value and EVA will be referenced in this book. It is not necessary to use economic value measurement techniques to reduce working capital and increase cash flow.

- **Economic value added (EVA)** is the return on total capital less the weighted average cost of capital (WACC) times the capital invested in the business. The computation of the weighted average cost of capital (WACC) is often debated. WACC is the market capitalization weighted average cost of equity plus the weighted after-tax cost of debt. The cost of equity is the premium for equities plus the long-term cost of risk-free debt adjusted for the risk of the company relative to the stock market (Beta.) In simple terms, the cost of equity has been 5% to 6% plus the ten-year Treasury bond interest rate times the company's Beta. If you are a private company you are probably wondering what this has to do with you. In a private company your shareholders should be receiving a return on investment commensurate with the return they would receive in the stock market for an investment in a stock of similar risk. If you have multiple private owners, measuring ROTC versus WACC is the only way you can truly measure performance of your company. See Appendices B and C for a full discussion and example of weighted average cost of capital and economic value added.

EVA is a measure of value creation in the business. If you present value all projected future EVA, you should have an approximation of market capitalization. You only create value when you earn above your cost of capital. Companies that have an ROTC above the cost of capital and are increasing EVA usually have rising stock prices. The EVA concept is very useful in helping management understand the economic trade-offs in managing a business. For example, it can be used to determine how much of a discount should be offered to reduce accounts receivable. Conversely, it can be used to determine when to accept a supplier discount to pay early or how much to pay for longer supplier terms. You can also examine tradeoffs between a higher cost of materials for smaller, more frequent deliveries and low inventory compared to low unit cost of materials ordered in large quantities and held for long periods in inventory. Use it in making decisions on reducing working capital. The WACC includes the cost of equity. It is very important to use the full cost of capital, including the cost of equity, when making working capital decisions. Treat the decision like a capital investment. Do not use only the cost of debt in making decisions on customer and supplier discounts.

Use accounting records for computation of financial measures

The data for the above measures can be taken directly from the accounting records. It does not have to be manipulated. No black box formula is required to compute or understand the financial measures. Best of all, the financial measures can be communicated to and understood by everyone from the shop floor to the boardroom.

Operational measures also required

There will be many operational measures such as orders filled on time, order fill rate, customer-requested delivery time met, invoice line accuracy, pricing accuracy and so forth. Focus on key operating measures of success from the customer's perspective. The customer may be an internal customer. You may have measures on which you think you are hitting 100%. However, if the customer measures you differently and you are only 70% on target by your customer's measure, then you are in trouble and need to take corrective action.

Chapter 6

VALUE CHAIN ANALYSIS

The value chain is the order-to-cash cycle

A major step in developing a working capital reduction program is to fully analyze and understand the company's value chain. The value chain is the complete order-to-cash cycle of the company. It is the entire set of processes involved in completing a sale to a customer, from acquiring the sale to depositing the cash in the bank. The revenue and purchasing processes must be analyzed to determine where time, cost, defects, non-value-added work and variation can be eliminated. All the processes must add value for the customer and for you. In addition, all processes must be fast and error-free for administrative, manufacturing, supply chain and finance activities. Reducing time and errors in the value chain will reduce working capital while also increasing customer service. It sounds simple to accomplish but it requires a focused effort to be successful.

Be rigorous in the evaluation of processes and people

People resistive to change will be the biggest obstacle to making fundamental improvements in your processes. Employees who want to hold on to old ideas and business practices and not carefully and honestly evaluate the usefulness and effectiveness of the processes they are using should work elsewhere. You have to be absolutely rigorous and honest in the evaluation of processes and people. Some long-term employees may have to leave your company. Treat them with dignity and respect, but they no longer have a function to fulfill in helping your company thrive in a highly competitive marketplace. If you don't improve your operations, some other company will do it for you when it takes over your business.

Map all processes in each functional area

To get started you should ask each functional area to map its end-to-end processes and note the cycle time for each part of the process. Don't allow any open loops to exist. Start with a sales lead and end with cash going into a bank account. This analysis will require hard work. Establish a war room. Put one person in charge. Hold regular meetings. Have targets for completion of tasks. Make people accountable for their part of the analysis.

Find opportunities to reduce cycle time

The value chain analysis gives you a map to locate the roadblocks that increase the order-fulfillment cycle time. You cannot mandate inventory reduction and reduced accounts receivable levels. Take defects out of manufacturing and shipping, reduce set-up time, speed up production lines, streamline product lines and simplify products. Complexity needs to be reduced to the extent possible. The more combinations and variations introduced into your product or processes, the more difficult it will be to have flexible, error-free and fast production and administration. Eliminating the defects and taking time out of the processes is very hard work and takes time. You may have to reorganize the layout of the plant and warehouse. That will cost money initially and require a new budget. The savings from reduced scrap, manufacturing costs, overhead and inventory obsolescence will pay for the plant and warehouse improvements many times over. If you are rigorous in your efforts you will find a factory in a factory that will allow you to grow substantially without adding manufacturing and warehouse space or equipment.

Value chain processes

The following top-level outline is a starting point for a company to use in organizing an end-to-end value chain process review. Develop detailed process maps for each function. This absolutely must be done before you start on a major working capital reduction program. The focus in this review is on the revenue cycle:

- Sales acquisition
- Pricing administration
- Order entry
- Credit control
- Order processing
- Order fulfillment
- Invoicing
- Materials management
- Logistics – shipping and receiving
- Purchasing
- Accounts payable
- Disbursement
- Manufacturing
- Accounts receivable management
- Collection
- Cash application
- Discrepancy management
- Bank deposit

The list of operations for your company will vary depending on the nature of your business. Underlying the process is the finance function with general ledger, fixed asset accounting and the financial analysis function. Other finance activities not on the list are tax and internal audit. The treasury function is assumed to be included in the disbursement and bank deposit activities.

Follow the order from inception to cash in the bank

The easiest way to get started on the value chain analysis is to follow an order as it is acquired until cash is in the bank. You can do the same for ordering materials. Follow the purchase order from inception until it is paid. You will find some activities that do not add any value to your customer. You will also find many process defects and activities that waste time. Ask the people doing the work to help you do the mapping. They know all the steps and which activities appear to be of no value or take an inordinate amount of time for value received, if any. These same people will also be a great source of ideas on how to improve processes.

Look for time delays, sources of errors and process variation. Reviewing the complaint log in the credit and collection department will show you what defects are being created in delivering a product to a customer. The major reasons customers don't pay an invoice are:

- No invoice received
- No proof of delivery
- No purchase order number on the invoice
- Wrong price and/or unit of measure
- Product damaged in shipping
- Product defects

Determining the major sources of defects and fixing the process errors that cause them will help you start to reduce working capital.

You are now ready to begin reducing working capital

Once you have completed the value chain analysis you are ready to begin the working capital reduction and cash flow improvement program. You should already have identified the quick fixes and begun attacking them before a formal program is underway. If you don't have to invest in working capital you can grow the business at great speed, assuming the fixed capital costs can be financed in the capital markets, leased or mortgage financed. That should be of great comfort to a fast-growing company. You will not have inventory on hand that isn't ordered and ultimately written off. You also won't have receivables that cannot be collected because they are old.

Chapter 7

TAKING ACTION

The easy work has been done. You are organized and you have mapped the value chain and analyzed financial performance and working capital over the past twenty quarters. Now comes the hard part–taking action to drive down working capital and reaching the long-term target of increased cash flow and reduced financing requirements.

By now you should have identified some easy quick fixes and perhaps have already started working on them. My recommendation is to pick the biggest opportunity and put your best people on it right away. You want to be able to show your team that it is possible to reduce working capital if you have a focused program. It may be as simple as designing new order entry procedures that eliminate order-entry errors or you may design a new invoice that makes it easier for the customer to find all the information required to pay on time. These improvements can be made without making major changes in the organization. These changes can produce results quickly by making the shipping of the correct product more streamlined with a correct invoice that is easy to process.

The chapters on each part of working capital are organized in the same sequence as a balance sheet. This does not mean you have to take action on them sequentially. As I stated earlier, you should attack the largest issues first. However, you need to complete the preparation work before proceeding too far on the improvement projects.

I have said many times that you will be working to drive time, defects, non-value-added work and variation out of all your processes. This is a continuous improvement program. You never stop making improvements to the value chain. The ultimate objective is outstanding customer service achieved by delivering a very high quality product on time with no administrative errors. Now you are ready to begin driving down working capital and increasing cash flow. If you can achieve this state of operational nirvana you will have a very robust company.

Chapter 8

CURRENT ASSET MANAGEMENT

Largest opportunity to reduce working capital and improve cash flow

Driving down current assets is critical to reducing working capital and increasing cash flow. Operating current assets averaged 33.5% of sales in the study I conducted. In most cases, operating current assets are 30% to 40% of sales while operating current liabilities are only 10% to 15% of sales. Accounts receivable and inventory are the main components of current assets. These are the two primary operating assets to carefully manage. They are linked, along with accounts payable, to the operations of the company. Managing operations to successfully drive down inventory will, in most cases, lead to better accounts receivable and accounts payable management. You can work on reducing accounts receivable and inventory at the same time. Avoid spreading your top people over too many projects. Pick the most urgent opportunities for improvement and focus on programs to fix the problems.

Start by reviewing the disputed item list

A good place to start reducing operating working capital is by analyzing the disputed item list in the accounts receivable collection department for the last six months. That list will tell you the reasons customers are not paying bills on time and what issues are creating customer dissatisfaction. Resolving the root causes of the most common disputed items is a great start to driving down working capital. For example, you may develop improved order entry procedures, install a better shipping program and reduce product defects. Fixing these issues will remove reasons not to pay on time. These issues probably surfaced in the value chain analysis and you may already be working on resolutions.

Reducing accounts receivable will be the most difficult task

Reducing accounts receivable is the hardest part of working capital management. No one wants to talk about reducing accounts receivable since that activity is viewed as negative. If you only set tough targets for your credit and collections department to achieve and increase the budget for collecting, you will have angry customers. Attacking the root causes of why customers don't pay on time will result in lower DSO, happier customers and improved cash flow. In some cases customers don't pay because strict enforcement of collection rules are not in place. If that is the case, educate your customers on your terms and conditions of sale, including on-time payment. A main aspect of receivables management is visiting the top twenty customers. Meet with your customers' accounts payable department and develop a working relationship to improve communication.

Good inventory management is critical

Inventory management is the heart of any good working capital management program. Installing a robust inventory management program requires that you introduce lean manufacturing techniques and get very close to your top twenty customers and suppliers. This is a considerable undertaking and cannot to be done without significant preparation and study. Inventory management needs to be customer-demand driven. The customer-demand data is used to set production schedules and order the delivery of raw materials.

Set targets and report on performance and include in compensation package

You can work on the other components of current assets while focusing on receivables and inventory. The key is to set targets for each area, report on them and include them in your compensation plan. Cash management is tied directly to accounts receivable and accounts payable management.

The person leading the cash balance reduction team needs to be involved with both the receivables and payables teams. Cash management is the beginning and end of the business cycle. You save time and money by properly managing the cash collection and disbursement processes.

As discussed earlier, don't overlook the smaller components of current assets. They are usually not well managed and can be reduced. Prepaid expenses and other receivables can be as much as 3% to 4% of sales. For a $10 million in sales company this can amount to an investment of $300,000 to $400,000. This is money hidden in the business that should be found and used to fund more strategic investments. These small balance sheet accounts should be managed.

Chapter 9

CASH MANAGEMENT

Cash is king

If you don't have enough cash to pay employees and suppliers you are out of business in a hurry. Maintaining an adequate strategic cash reserve, bank credit line or access to cash from whatever source is critical to managing a business. Without adequate cash flow and/or access to capital you cannot grow your business. Increasing cash flow and minimizing the amount of investment required to grow the business is therefore a strategic imperative.

Cash touches every part of the business

Cash is an integral part of the revenue and expense cycle. It should be part of every balance sheet for performance measurement purposes. Cash touches all aspects of the business and needs to be carefully managed in order to minimize investment in the business.

Two types of cash: operational and strategic

There are two types of cash: operational and strategic. Operating cash is used to run the day-to-day operations of the business. Strategic cash is held to meet specific strategic objectives of the business. The strategic objective can be to buffer the business against volatile business conditions, which can create highly fluctuating cash flows and earnings patterns or to pay for a large capital expenditure or an acquisition. Planning for financial crises before they occur will require some careful thought and analysis. For example, many companies were not prepared for the October 2008 financial collapse. I believe that you can determine optimal levels of strategic cash and/or credit lines that will allow you to weather these financial storms.

Minimizing cash can significantly increase cash flow and the return on capital

Minimizing operating cash balances is very important. In the study of fifteen manufacturing companies, total cash as a percentage of sales averaged 15.7% and ranged from 2% to 50%. The average equates to nearly two months of sales in cash. There was no clear distinction between cash held for strategic purposes and cash used to operate the business. Cash is clearly a major investment in many businesses. There are very few investments or cost-saving initiatives as easy and inexpensive to accomplish as installing improved cash management procedures. This activity can generate increased cash flow and reduce costs. Improving cash management and driving operating cash to zero requires a modest effort with almost no risk and little or no investment. It does, however, require a change in philosophy and attitude toward financial risk management. If this is the only concept you use from this book, you will have made a significant contribution to your company.

Large cash balances can be a crutch for management

Large cash balances are often used as a crutch for poor strategic planning or management of the business. Often senior management does not want to give the cash back to the shareholders. If there is no long-term plan for using the cash in the business, it should be returned to the shareholders either through a dividend or by repurchasing shares. Excess cash often inspires management to take business risks it might not otherwise take. Large cash balances are also used as a safety net so management can stand in front of the shareholders and claim it can ride out any economic storm. Management should be able to plan how to navigate through all types of economic environments without using excess cash. That is what management is paid to accomplish. It shouldn't use shareholder cash as a crutch for poor planning and execution.

Zero operating cash is achievable

Most businesses have predictable cash flow cycles and earning streams and can plan for the amount of operating cash required. If the business is borrowing, borrow only what is needed each day. This is similar to inventory management. The manufacturing philosophy should be to make and ship only what is sold every day. If the business has excess operating cash that cannot be used to repay debt, set up a program to invest all cash not needed to operate the business each day. Banks have the ability to invest excess cash in a bank account on a daily basis. These types of banking arrangements are called sweep accounts. The downside is that the interest paid on these types of accounts is very low so sweep account balances should be minimized. The longer the term of investment, the higher the rate of interest paid unless the interest rate, or yield curve as it is called in finance circles, is inverted (short-term interest rates higher than long-term interest rates) or very low and flat, and that rarely occurs.

Review cash balances relative to debt

An additional consideration to take into account when reviewing cash management is the level of cash relative to debt. Many of the companies I have analyzed have had significant amounts of debt while at the same time have excess operating cash. Excluding the companies that had no long-term debt, short-term debt as a percentage of total debt was only 10.7%. Interestingly, short-term debt as a percentage of sales averaged only 2.8% and ranged from a high of 9% to a low of 0%. In fact, the average amount of short-term debt is only about one and one-half weeks of sales. These companies routinely generated cash that could not be used to pay down debt and was invested at rates significantly lower than the cost of long-term debt and the cost of capital. These companies consistently reduce net income and destroy economic value year after year for no apparent reason by borrowing while at the same time having excess cash. The cash should have been used to reduce debt or returned to shareholders. Even in difficult economic periods the companies continued to have massive amounts of excess cash while still borrowing. There appeared to be no business rationale to maintain all the excess cash except to allow operating management to sleep better at night. In many instances the companies with excess cash only had expensive long-term debt that could not be repaid. This is a very sad situation, particularly for the shareholders.

Excess operating cash destroys value

A very young, brash and bright division finance executive once told a group of his contemporaries that he thought excess operating cash was evil. It was a bit of an overstatement, but not far from the truth. A corporation does not need any excess operating cash. Excess operating cash is a wasting asset. It creates no economic value unless it is held for a very specific strategic reason. Cash destroys economic value since you cannot possibly invest cash prudently at a yield equal to your cost of capital. Think of cash as similar to physical inventory. You should have only as much operating cash as you absolutely need to run the business and that is zero, in my opinion, for most businesses. You can balance the net of the out-flow and in-flow of cash each day with changes in short-term borrowing. I did this for decades and it worked perfectly. The prudent use of short-term debt allows the company to eliminate operating cash.

Cash management is more than a treasury matter

Cash is often excluded from working capital management programs. It is assumed to be a treasury issue and not part of operations. The management of cash is left to treasury and not included in the operating team performance measures for return on capital. However, the operating team can heavily influence cash flow and cash balances by the way it requires customers to pay and establishes procedures to pay vendors. Management teams that do not include cash as part of working capital are missing a big opportunity to minimize cash used in the business, thus foregoing an opportunity to further increase return on capital and increase cash flow. Unless operating cash is included on the operating company balance sheet, you cannot get management to develop programs to reduce cash balances. Large cash balances can result from financing and operating decisions such as inter-company payment terms and inter-company loans. This is particularly true in foreign operations where government rules and regulations can often make cash movements out of or into the country very difficult. If you have excess cash in a foreign country, it may be extremely expensive to repatriate cash to the U.S. parent company due to U.S. income taxes. It may be difficult to repatriate cash in foreign operations due to local regulations. Because of government regulations, Eastman Kodak had 30% of its cash in China when it filed for bankruptcy. Many companies with over-capitalized foreign subsidiaries have large cash balances in countries with depreciating currencies. You do not want to be in that situation.

Managing cash is risky and time-consuming

All cash investments require extensive effort and cost to be properly managed and controlled. In the average large corporate treasury department, one third of all activity is focused on controlling and managing cash investments. This is a costly, risky and time-consuming exercise. Having large cash balances to manage diverts treasury department attention away from productive activity such as reducing interest expense, managing foreign currency exposure, optimizing the cash-gathering and disbursing system, optimizing the capital structure of the firm and minimizing working capital invested in the business. The last two activities add significant value to the firm at a nominal cost and a low risk while managing cash investments is risky business. Therefore, any operating cash balances should be minimized or preferably eliminated and strategic cash balances should be only large enough to meet planned strategic objectives.

Many companies with relatively stable earnings and cash flow continually maintain very high cash balances. They tell shareholders every year that they need large cash balances for strategic purposes such as acquisitions. Even after making acquisitions each year they still have large cash balances. This decreases economic value by increasing invested capital which is then invested and earning returns below the weighted average cost of capital.

Determine the amount of strategic cash required by the level of business risk

A way to conceptually think about the appropriate level of cash required to operate a business is to relate operating income and/or cash-flow volatility as a percentage of sales to cash as a percentage of sales. Using this analytical framework, you can categorize companies into one of four major groupings. The following chart graphically represents this analysis. You need high cash balances if the business is risky and low cash balances if the business is stable. Although this seems intuitively obvious, most companies do not follow this approach in establishing a cash balance strategy.

Amount of strategic cash required is a function of business risk

Cash as a % of sales	Low	High
High	Avoid high cash balances in low-risk businesses	High-risk businesses need large strategic cash balances
Low	Low cash balances add value by reducing invested capital	Avoid low cash balances in high-risk business

Operating income and/or cash flow volatility as a percentage of sales

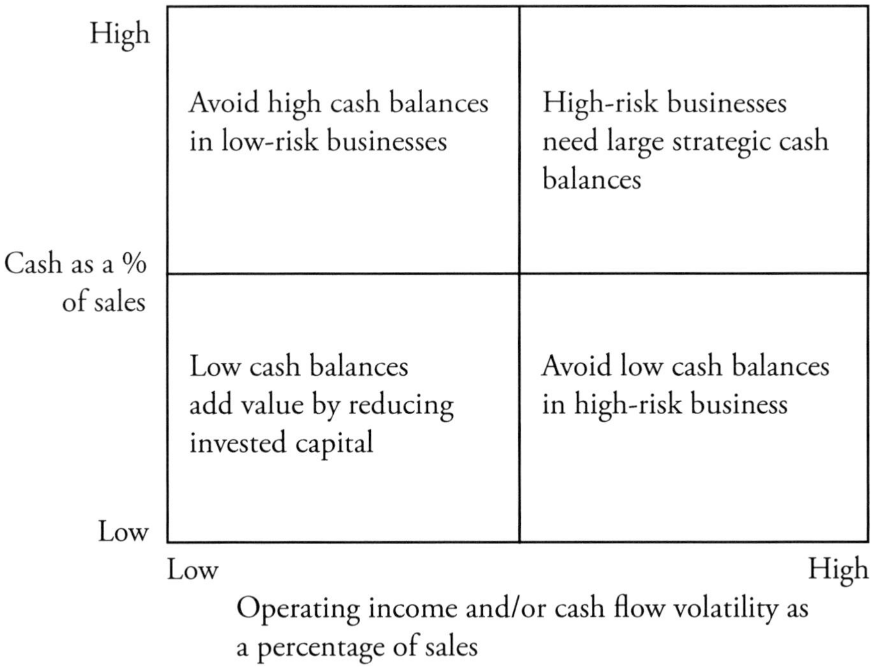

The amount of cash required to operate a business is a function of business risk and strategy. Highly risky businesses need cash reserves to fund possible periods of negative cash flow and operating losses. A business

may also be growing by acquisition and want to have significant cash balances to fund part or all of the planned acquisitions. Businesses with low cash flow and earnings volatility need zero operating cash even if they have an acquisition program. Credit lines can be established to fund acquisitions for companies with stable earnings and cash flow streams.

Strategic planning process should determine business risk

The actual level of cash needed to run the business should be determined in the strategic planning process and is a function of cash flow and business risk. In periods of negative cash flow and losses, financial institutions will not lend to a company or, if they do, only under onerous terms. They also will not want to make loans or lend at a reasonable cost for certain types of acquisitions. Banks want to be repaid and in many instances only make credit available to companies that don't need the credit line. The critical issue to examine in determining what level of strategic cash to maintain is established by how large and stable your company is and the strength of your position in your industry. Assess your strength and position with your financial institutions. The Great Recession of 2008 and 2009 gives many companies an idea of the worst-case scenario to plan for in terms of negative cash flow as well as worst-case operating financing requirements.

Strategic planning should determine the amount of cash reserves required for business investment or to fund operations in difficult business periods. This is a finance decision to be made with input from senior operating management and the board of directors.

An excess cash investment policy is needed

The excess cash investment policy should be based on safety, liquidity and yield, in that order. Do not deviate from that policy. Many treasurers get caught in risky investments that end up in large losses while trying to maximize yield, forgetting that their job is to protect assets. The significant investment losses incurred several years ago by a number of large companies were caused by investing in interest rate and currency derivative products and speculating on stock market, interest rate and currency movements. The treasury people were mesmerized by the returns but did not understand the financial instruments and inherent risks. When the financial markets became unstable, they could not sell their exotic financial instruments and huge losses were incurred. If you don't understand the financial product, don't invest in it. If properly invested, the funds will be available when needed, given a reasonable amount of advance notice. No funds will be lost and the yield will be greater than what is available on a sweep bank account.

The cash management program recommended in this book requires a robust cash management structure and excellent bank relations. It also requires a debt management strategy that reflects the risks in the business. Cash truly is a shared responsibility between operations and treasury. It is the integration of business planning and execution and cash and debt management that enables a business to minimize cash. If the company is borrowing, it can refinance a portion of its debt every day either by increasing or decreasing the amount of debt depending on the daily cash flow. Since overnight financing is available to large corporations, a portion of short-term debt can be maintained on an overnight basis to manage short-term fluctuations in cash flow.

Even if overnight financing is not available you can borrow or pay down bank debt every day. In many cases this can be done via the Internet. It can be done if you are a $5,000,000 or $500,000,000 sales company. The key is to be organized and have a process in place to manage the cash program.

Cash and short-term debt management strategies are linked

The cash management strategy is linked closely to the debt management strategy. The amount of short-term debt a company can manage is a function of projected cash flow and earnings fluctuation over a yearly or business cycle. The minimum amount of short-term debt is the amount required to maintain the company in a borrowing position at all times. This eliminates any excess operating cash. A company needs enough short-term borrowing to manage the cash-flow cycle of the business and avoid excess operating cash. For example, if the cumulative monthly cash flow varies from a positive $100,000 balance to a low of a negative $100,000 balance, the minimum amount of short-term debt should be at least $100,000 to eliminate any excess cash. In this case the maximum amount of short-term debt would be $200,000. Furthermore, if the company generates $100,000 of positive cash flow from operations after capital expenditures each year, the minimum short-term borrowings should range from $200,000 to a maximum of $300,000 to avoid excess cash before any dividends, long-term debt repayments or acquisition financing.

When determining the amount of short-term floating-rate debt, consider the potential impact of changes in short-term interest rates on the earnings of the company, the level of interest relative to EBIT and the accounting working capital amount. You do not want to have the short-term debt management strategy put the earnings and cash flow stream at risk. You also do not want short-term debt to put the company in a negative accounting working capital position.

A prudent approach is to have the potential impact on earnings from interest rate changes be less than 3% of EBIT (operating income.) You can choose a higher or lower number but it should be 5% or less. In all but a very few cases short-term interest rates have risen less than an absolute 3% in any twelve month period. In fact, short-term interest rates rarely move more than an absolute 4% over any two-year period. Thus, 3% times EBIT divided by 4% gives you a very conservative maximum level of short-term debt you can incur and avoid a significant impact on earnings from increases in interest rates. Make sure that the absolute level of interest expense does not put the company at risk. Interest coverage of ten times EBIT is prudent, assuming EBIT is relatively stable.

Do your own analysis of interest rate volatility and EBIT volatility before concluding the maximum amount of short-term debt your company can prudently utilize. For example, if EBIT is $1 million, 3% of EBIT is $30,000 which, divided by 4%, is $750,000 and is the maximum amount of short-term floating rate debt that would be prudent assuming the EBIT stream is stable. If EBIT varies plus or minus 20%, you should reduce the maximum borrowing level by 20% to avoid earnings and cash flow issues in difficult economic periods.

Be sure the amount of short-term debt does not give rise to negative working capital when measured on an accounting basis. In my example, a company with $1 million in EBIT would likely have sales of $10 million and operating working capital as a percentage of sales of about 22%, or $2.2 million. Thus, short-term debt of $750,000 would not put the company in a negative working capital position on an accounting basis. You can stress test your maximum level of short-term debt using this analytical approach. Before engaging in any short- term debt program you should thoroughly review the matter with your accountants and bankers to get their input and advice.

Based on my experience, most companies and banks do not prepare this type of analysis. Thus, most companies have too much fixed rate long-term debt or rely on too much equity capital. Many companies have excess cash invested short- term at low rates but also have long-term debt that is not pre-payable and is costing more than the short-term investments are yielding. This is just poor financial planning and execution. This strategy reduces economic value and reduces earnings. With planning, a company can manage cash flow and economic risk and not have huge excess cash balances essentially funded by expensive long-term debt.

Every company should have a short-term credit line and use short-term debt to manage cash flow. Using my analytical approach, a $10 million in sales company with $1 million in EBIT can have a $750,000 million short-term credit line. If the absolute interest rate were 5%, then maximum annual interest expense would be $37,500. This would equate to interest coverage of 26.7, which means EBIT is 26.7 times greater than interest expense. Even if short-term interest rates rose to 10% and EBIT declined 20%, the minimum interest coverage would be 10.7, which is still very prudent. This type of financial stress testing is important to ensure you do not overly leverage the company with short-term debt. The actual amount of short-term borrowing required would be determined by the yearly cash flow cycle. If cash flow as a percentage of sales is 3%, then in one year cash flow would be 40% of short-term debt and could be paid off in two and one-half years.

This is just a very quick example of an approach to take in determining how much short-term floating rate debt a company can consider borrowing. There are many factors to consider. Carefully review your business risks including interest coverage, cash flow, balance sheet structure, the economic outlook, competitive situation, industry outlook, interest rate trends and projected financial position in determining a financing strategy.

In order to achieve zero operating cash you must establish a cash management function and designate someone to oversee that activity. In larger companies a treasurer is appointed. In smaller companies the cash management function is placed in the controllers department. In all cases you must have a specific person or group of people identified who are responsible every day for managing cash. You cannot miss a debt repayment or an interest payment. You need a solid organization with very reliable people.

Along with good people you need a good bank with expertise in cash management to assist you in carrying out an efficient cash management program. If the bank does not have a strong program in cash management, find one that does. The bank should have the technical capability, systems and service to make cash management easy for you as wcll as lending capability. With on-line banking, the cash management program I advocate should be easy to install. Internet banking makes it possible to manage all basic transactions from your office.

Key steps to cash management success

The following are recommended steps to establish a basic cash management program. Your bank should help you refine this program as technology changes over time.

- **Establish a cash management function**
  Appoint someone who is very responsible and will perform the activity every day. Make sure there is a backup for this person.

- **Select a strong bank for cash management**
  Meet with your existing bank. If it cannot meet your needs for managing a robust cash management program, start looking for a new bank. You want an Internet-based system that will allow you to manage the cash position on line. Automate payments and receipts to the extent possible. Your bank should be able to do this for you.

- **Establish cash management policies and procedures**
  Include all the basic policies and procedures outlined in this chapter.

- **Monitor cash balances in the bank every day**
  Start to track daily in-flows, out-flows and balances. You will need to know the cash cycle of the company to be able to determine the amount of a short-term debt credit line.

- **Establish a bank credit line sufficient to allow you to keep the company in a borrowing position all the times**
  Make sure you can use it on a daily basis for borrowing or repayment.

- **Deposit all receipts into one account**
  Ask large customers to pay electronically directly into your collection account. Move all good funds from this account to a concentration account to pay disbursements. Make sure you can integrate your electronic payments into your accounting system. Establish a lockbox collection account with your bank if it is economically feasible. This allows payments by check to go directly to the bank.

- **Make all disbursements from one account**
  By not mixing receipts and disbursements, transactions can easily be identified and accounts can be reconciled quickly. Separating the receipt and disbursement accounts also allows for separation of duties, which provides better internal control.

- **Concentrate all cash in one account**
  Use the concentration account to fund the disbursement account.

Borrow the net required each day in this account. Invest the excess cash in short-term deposits or use it to reduce short-term debt. You do not need a concentration account if you only have one collection and one disbursing account. In this case, the collection account can act as the concentration account.

- **Close all petty cash accounts**
  Do not allow any petty cash accounts. Use purchasing cards and expense accounts to fund miscellaneous small expenses. Petty cash accounts are no longer necessary with the advent of purchasing cards, expense account cards and universal ATM machines. Petty cash accounts are a source of possible abuse and theft. Using the expense account system avoids the issue of managing actual cash.

- **Use direct payroll deposit and a payroll company to manage payroll**
  Managing payroll checks is very labor intensive and costly. This activity can be outsourced. If possible, all payrolls should be direct deposit. If employees do not have bank accounts, issue them purchasing cards that can be reloaded each payday.

- **Minimize the number of bank accounts**
  Be very rigid on this rule. If you have several plants, you may encounter resistance to the change. Plants do not need bank accounts. With purchasing and expense account cards, ATMs and express mail, the need for check-writing capability has been eliminated. Close all accounts not absolutely needed to operate the business. Eliminate the small plant bank accounts. Much of the fraud I have seen involved these type of small bank accounts. There were insufficient people to perform good internal control. In most fraud cases, a very trusted employee committed the crime.

- **Prepare an excess cash investment policy**
  As discussed above, it is critical to make sure any excess cash is properly managed.

- **Arrange a sweep account to invest any excess cash**
  Thus, any excess cash is automatically invested at the end of the day.

- **Start a purchasing card program for small-value purchases**
  Major credit card companies have purchasing card programs. This eliminates the need for petty cash and can be used to increase control of spending.

- **Accept purchasing cards for small-value sales**
  Have a purchasing card program tied into your accounting system. The major card companies and/or your bank can assist you in establishing a program. Be aggressive in asking customers to pay for small-value purchases with a purchasing card. With the rapid growth of company purchasing card programs, it should be easy to install one for your business. As I will discuss in the chapter on accounts receivable management, a purchasing card program can be very helpful in collection work and in accepting new customers.

You may meet resistance to closing plant bank accounts, eliminating petty cash accounts and using purchasing cards, ATMs and expense accounts for small cash needs. The purpose of the program is to improve cash controls by reducing the number of bank accounts, cash locations and transactions going through bank accounts and the accounts payable and receivables departments. The goal is to automate and simplify the entire cash gathering and disbursing system. By automating the cash gathering and disbursing system and simplifying the accounts receivable and accounts payable processes you can significantly reduce staffing in these departments and eliminate the need for costly and complex remote outsourcing services for these activities. Eliminate the complexity associated with checks and multiple bank accounts. Replace them with electronic transactions and highly secure purchasing card transactions both for purchases and sales. The key is to use the Internet and purchasing cards as much as possible to process transactions.

Purchasing cards should be used to reduce complexity and increase control

Expense account reimbursement cards are the employee's responsibility. They can be used to obtain cash from ATM machines. These cards can be issued to people in remote locations. They can be used, along with purchasing cards, to eliminate petty cash and local bank accounts.

Purchasing cards are the responsibility of the company but the employee should be required to sign a statement taking responsibility for using the card according to company policy. Card usage can be blocked to allow transactions only with specific vendor codes and a maximum specific dollar amount per purchase and in total. A supervisor should be required to sign the statement each month and the statements should be reviewed in a central location. Reports on purchases by vendors can be obtained from the card company. This data can be used in vendor negotiations. It is a very powerful purchasing tool. The card company can also supply monthly data to update expense reporting. Work with the card vendor to establish a program that fits your needs. The purchasing card eliminates the need for many small transactions being processed through accounts payable. It also reduces the number of transactions through the bank account. At the same time, purchasing cards can give the company greater control over spending with pre-established expense limits and specified vendors.

Summary

Improving cash management may seem like a lot of work for such a seemingly small impact on cash flow and working capital. However, the benefits from installing a robust cash management system in terms of cost savings from better cash control and reduced transactions to reduce cash balances make this program very powerful. Managing the cash flow of the company in a prudent yet aggressive manner will reduce the invested capital of the company and increase cash flow. It will also reduce costs and reduce risk. Automating and reducing the number of transactions will reduce the time required to collect and pay invoices.

Installing a comprehensive cash management program will impact all aspects of the company from collections to payments. Do not underestimate the resistance you will encounter in attempting to install many of the programs, particularly from operations. Your board of directors will also need considerable explanation before they approve a zero operating cash program. This is not a routine change in the way to manage cash flow. However, do not waiver from working to install a very robust cash management program. A new cash management program can be the starting point for an aggressive working capital reduction program. Remember, cash touches every part of the operation of a company.

Chapter 10

ACCOUNTS RECEIVABLE MANAGEMENT

A big opportunity

Accounts receivable is usually one of the biggest opportunities for working capital reduction and improved cash flow. It is very difficult to reduce accounts receivable successfully. However, positive programs to reduce accounts receivable can be installed that will improve customer service. In the study of fifteen manufacturing companies, DSO ranged from 23.6 to 100.9 days with an average of 59.7 days or 16.4% of sales. Accounts receivable is almost always the largest component of working capital. Only rarely is inventory larger than accounts receivable. In my study, inventory turnover was 5.6, or 12.5% of sales.

Receivables management directly touches the customer and can be used to develop an enhanced positive relationship. Usually nothing substantive is accomplished in a receivables reduction program because no one wants to tell a slow-paying customer to pay on time or ask a customer to pay faster with shorter credit terms. However, it has been my experience that if you develop programs to improve customer service by reducing the customer's working capital and operating costs, the customer will work with you on faster payment. It takes courage to establish such programs but they can work and achieve large benefits for your customer and you.

Make it easy for customers to pay quickly

The objective of accounts receivable management should be to make it very easy for a customer to pay quickly. Most accounts receivable management programs do not follow this philosophy. The focus of most programs is on the ability of the customer to ultimately pay and to avoid bad-debt losses. Having the customer pay faster actually reduces the risk of a bad-debt loss.

Other than reducing sales, there are only two ways to reduce accounts receivable: reduce credit terms and/or reduce past-due receivables. Making it easy for the customer to pay quickly sounds very simple but it is not. In order for a customer to pay faster, a change in the payment process is usually required. Companies put many obstacles in the way for the customer to pay quickly. Billing and shipping errors cause the customer to delay payment until the errors are corrected. Treating credit and collections as a service organization focused on making it easy for the customer to pay quickly is a very different approach from how most credit and collection departments are managed. You may have people responsible for managing accounts receivable who do not want to change the credit and collection processes or their attitude and approach to the customer. If that is the case you must change the personnel first before moving forward. Getting buy-in from the accounts receivable, finance and sales teams for the new approach to managing accounts receivable is critical to success.

Over the years, I have sometimes had the impression that credit managers see the customer as the enemy. I am sure the sales and marketing departments, in many instances, view the credit department as a sales prevention organization. This is particularly true when credit and collections turns down a request to sell to a customer. The issue usually is that the sales and marketing people are not focused on selling to credit-worthy customers. They do not have sales and marketing plans that target companies with good payment histories and financial strength. My credit philosophy has been to find customers who pay on time, are profitable, and focus on sales and service to those customers while an aggressive credit policy is put in place. Conversely, work to eliminate the slow-paying, unprofitable accounts.

Sales and finance must work together

In order to develop a comprehensive accounts receivable management program that includes reduced credit term arrangements, the sales and credit management departments must work together. The sales force usually does not want to talk about credit and collections with the customer and does not want anyone from finance meeting with their customer. However, this has to be done in order to have an effective accounts receivable management program. Your sales force may tell you that the competitors are giving credit terms much longer than yours and not enforcing them. You can only verify this information by being active with customers and credit associations. Your credit and collection department touches your customer as much, if not more, than the sales department. Sales and finance need to work closely together to make sure the customer's needs are being fully met not only in delivering the right defect-free product on time but also administratively from invoicing to collection.

Customers pay but often not on time

It is my experience that customers almost always pay. They just don't always pay on time. Bad debts are typically very low, usually less than ¼% to ½% of sales. The issue is getting the customer to pay on time. Customers use a variety of excuses to not pay within stated credit terms. Make sure you are very clear with your customer about your collection expectations. If you delivery a high-quality product on time with no administrative or shipping errors, you should expect to be paid within credit terms. This philosophy needs to be communicated to your customer and reinforced periodically by the sales force. Credit extension and payment on time are part of the selling proposition. It is not a sale until payment is collected. Many people in big companies are isolated from actual cash flow and are not even aware of the collection issue. However, I can assure you that cash flow and late-paying customers are always at the top of a small businessperson's list of issues. Time after time when I ask small business owners about their business, they invariably respond that sales are all right but collections could be better. If prompt collection of invoices is important to business survival in a small business then receivables collection should not diminish in importance in a large company.

An example of how not to manage accounts receivable

The following is an actual example of how a non-customer-centric credit and collections department drove away a long-term customer. The customer was experiencing a temporary cash flow problem and had to pay salaries before he paid his supplier. This resulted in the supplier's credit department holding up shipment on an order for parts that were critical tor the completion of a product. The supplier's credit department did not tell the customer that the shipment had been stopped. When the customer called to determine the status of the order he was told that he had not paid his past-due invoices and therefore the new order had not been shipped. Although the customer said that a check was in the mail, the credit manager refused to release the order until it arrived. Even though the customer had previously paid almost every invoice on time and had kept promises made, the supplier's salesperson could not override the credit department's policy.

I advised the customer to ask the supplier's credit department if it would accept a credit card payment and the credit department agreed to this action. My guess is that they would also have accepted a bank wire transfer. My client used a purchasing card and stopped payment on the mailed check. The supplier was technically right in not shipping to the customer with the unpaid invoice but the reason for non-shipment of the order was not communicated and the customer was not offered a payment alternative. Additionally, the supplier did not take into account past performance of the customer. Consequently, the customer felt poorly treated and decided to look for a new parts supplier.

The morale of the story is to make sure your credit and collections department or, better yet, the customer financial services department, uses creativity and flexibility in administering a credit policy. Above all else, make sure the lines of communication between the company and the customer are open. The credit department in the example administered a set of rules that lacked flexibility and creativity. It focused only on meeting credit department rules and did not see the bigger picture of helping a long-term customer. There were no alternative payment options offered. The supplier did not make it easy for the customer to pay quickly. There was no coordination between sales and credit and collections. What appeared on paper to be a solid, conservative credit and collections policy resulted in a long-term customer taking his business to another supplier.

Two basic parts to credit management

There are two basic aspects to accounts receivable management: granting and enforcing a credit line and collecting past-due balances. The purpose of the policies for establishing credit terms and the amount of a customer credit line should be to facilitate profitable sales. The policies should be developed taking into account the customer base and industry. Do not make the policies and procedures too cumbersome or difficult to understand. These policies must be communicated to the sales force and the customer. If the policies are onerous and complicated they will be ignored. Having a good credit-granting policy should reduce the number of past-due balances and time spent on collecting them.

Action steps to reduce accounts receivable

- Establish the leadership team.
- Set performance measures and targets.
- Change the name of the credit and collections department to the customer financial services department.
- Map the order-to-payment cycle.
- Analyze the current accounts receivable situation.
- Have correct customer data in the customer master file.
- Involve the sales force in the program.
- Focus on the top twenty customers.
- Settle customer disputes and claims very quickly.
- Establish a credit term policy.
- Establish a credit line policy.

- Renegotiate credit terms with key customers.
- Set fair credit and collection rules and follow them.
- Automate the collection process to the extent possible.
- Prepare a credit and collections policy and procedures manual.
- Establish a rigorous training program for sales and customer financial services on managing accounts receivable.

This may seem like a daunting list of tasks but the work can be done over time. You probably have completed many of the steps or only need to revise existing policies and procedures to fit the new approach to credit and collections. Many of the tasks can be done in parallel. Start by organizing a team to reduce accounts receivable with the objective of making it easy for a customer to pay quickly. Focus on the top twenty customers, making it a policy to have someone from the finance team visit the customers' accounts payable department. Minimize disputed items and settle them very quickly, negotiate shorter credit terms for key customers and automate the collection process to speed up collection of accounts receivable. As a result, you will have improved customer service.

Establish the leadership team

The logical choice for a leader is the top finance person. However, my suggestion is to make the CEO or COO the leader of this team. Other good candidates are the head of operations and the head of sales and marketing. Accounts receivable management is much larger than finance and is an operating issue. The team should consist of sales, marketing, manufacturing, logistics and finance, including a person from accounts receivable accounting and management. The key is to put action-oriented change agents on the team. Old thinking will not work. Reducing accounts receivable is a very tough part of working capital reduction. You need a very strong leader and team. The general attitude of many employees in the company will be that if bad debt losses are low, don't rock the boat by trying to get customers to pay faster. In reality they are missing a great opportunity to improve customer service and, in so doing, gain more of the customer's business. If you make it easier for the customer to pay, you will be taking time, defects and variation out of the processes, thereby lowering the cost of doing business. If the team has proper incentives, members will find many ways to reduce accounts receivable while at the same time improving customer service.

Set the following performance measures and targets

- DSO net, gross and DSO current within terms
- Aging of accounts receivable by due date as follows:
  - Percent of receivables within terms
  - Percent of receivables 1 to 15 days past due
  - Percent of receivables 16 to 30 days past due
  - Percent of receivables 31 to 60 days past due
  - Percent of receivables 61 to 90 days past due
  - Percent of receivables 91 days or more past due
  - Percent of receivables disputed
- Bad debt amount and also as a % of sales
- Average time to settle disputed items
- Monthly collection target based on previous month sales

Report these measures monthly showing the month (and year-to-date as appropriate) compared with the prior year's results.

Measuring DSO gross and DSO current are the two basic measurement tools for credit and collection. DSO gross, excluding bad debt and returns and allowances reserves, shows how fast, on average, your customer is paying. Benchmark this against competitors, customers and suppliers to the extent the data is available. You may have to deduct reserves for the external comparison since that is how your competitors, customers and suppliers will report the data externally. DSO current within terms is an approximation of the weighted average credit terms. It will quickly tell you if terms extensions are being granted. Benchmark DSO current against a computed weighted average credit term based on previous sales history. Don't let the team fall into the trap of spending countless hours debating thc calculation method. Set a reasonable calculation method for DSO and stick with it. Study and analyze the trend and absolute level of DSO.

I have seen receivable agings that age past due receivables 91 to 120, 121 to 150 and so on. Any invoice more than 90 days past due is either a dispute that will not be easily resolved or a bad debt. Make sure that almost no invoices are 91 days or more past due.

The percentage of receivables in dispute and the amount of bad debts and bad debts as a percentage of sales are very good indicators of the health of your receivables management program and your customer base. Look at the trend of the numbers as well as the absolute level. In general you should find that bad debts as a percentage of sales are very low, usually less than ½ % of sales. Unfortunately, the focus of most credit departments tends to be on avoiding bad debts rather than trying to get customers to pay on time.

Your finance team can develop many more measures, but in my experience these are the critical measures to review monthly. For standards, you should benchmark DSO against other companies in your industry focusing on your direct competitors. The National Association of Credit Managers has data on credit terms and DSO by industry. Your customer financial services manager will also probably belong to a trade association that shares useful data. Benchmarking is important but use the data carefully. It will tell you the conventional wisdom within the industry yet it may not point out the best ways to serve your customer.

Setting standards is not easy, but you need a target for percent current. My suggestion is to set a target of 95% current within terms, 4% past due 1 to 30 days, and 1% over 30 days past due. About 3% of receivables should be in the 1 to 15 days past due category. In other words, only 2% of sales should be more than 15 days past due. Examine the aging report that categorizes a company's accounts receivable according to the length of time an invoice has been outstanding. Any aging not achieving the targets for percent current and percent past due will tell you there are issues to be resolved.

Change the name of the credit and collection department

The credit and collections department should be called the customer financial services department. The message is that the department can provide the customers with assistance to pay on time. That means ensuring that a correct invoice is delivered very quickly with enough correct information to pay it. Show the due date, what was purchased and the purchase order number, if required. The information on what was purchased must make sense to the customer. If he believes he bought 500 red widgets then the invoice should state that information along with the customer part number. I have thrown invoices away that contain a lot of supplier information but never stated in understandable language what was purchased.

Map the order-to-payment cycle

A major step in starting to improve accounts receivable management is to map the order-to-payment cycle in great detail. If you have not done this in the value chain analysis, do it now. The person in charge of accounts receivable management should do this work with the help of an analyst. If the mapping has been completed it should be reviewed from a credit and collections point of view. This analysis will show you where you can take time, non-value-added work and errors out of the process so the customer can pay within stated credit terms. Once you understand the order-to-cash cycle you can start to reduce accounts receivable. Before you say you can't eliminate or at least substantially reduce receivables, take another look. It can be done. I have seen it done many times in many different countries and in a variety of industries.

Analyze the current accounts receivable situation

In addition to the order-to-cash map prepared as part of the value chain analysis, review the following information as soon as possible. Out of the details will come some quick-hit ideas. Based on my experience, I believe you will find that customers ultimately pay you but not on time. If your systems cannot generate the following data, do some systems work to gather the information.

- **Age accounts receivable per the aging structure shown in descending order by value by customer**
  Include DSO total and DSO current. Also show year-to-date or trailing twelve months sales for each customer. From this listing, the top twenty customers will be apparent. This is the group of customers to visit and then determine how to have them pay faster. You may want to segment customers by channel of distribution or type. The key is to have a relevant segmentation of customers in order of importance. If possible, include customer credit terms in the aging list. You can then compare credit terms with total DSO by customer and in total.

- **List all credit terms**
  You will be amazed by the extensive variety of credit terms that are currently being granted. This has occurred over time resulting from special deals made with customers. Those special deals became the norm and now you are stuck with them, or so your sales force tells you. Renegotiate credit terms that are longer than the standard.

- **List all disputes by type and amount over the last twelve months**
  My guess is that the disputes, listed in order of value, will be:

  No invoice received
  Wrong price and/or unit of measure on the invoice
  No purchase order number on the invoice
  No proof of delivery
  Damaged goods
  Short shipment
  Defective product

  All of these errors can be corrected. Most of the disputes are caused by administrative errors. Improving administrative processes for sales and order entry along with sales and order entry personnel training can eliminate most errors that are disputed items. Focus on the errors that are causing the most trouble and fix them. Separate the disputes into type with a dollar amount for each dispute, and then determine totals for each type of dispute. The disputed item analysis, along with the order-to-cash map, is the best starting point for establishing a working capital reduction program. It will tell you very quickly what issues are creating customer ill will and causing slow pay. This analysis can also be used by manufacturing and logistics in designing inventory improvement programs. If you correct the errors you definitely will be improving customer service and eliminate obstacles for the customer to pay on time.

- **Review the invoice information and layout**

Here is a quick test to give to your invoicing and/or finance team. Ask members to identify all the information on the invoice and explain why it is needed in order for the customer to pay. Also ask the team to tell you the payment due date based on an actual invoice. I have never had anyone pass the test with 100% correct answers. In fact, often a group of ten usually can only give me 60% to 70% of the information.

The invoice you are currently using will probably have to be redesigned. I have heard managers say they just ordered a large batch of invoices and have to use them before creating and ordering a new invoice. That is bad logic. Invoices are inexpensive relative to the investment in accounts receivable. Most invoices I have observed are poorly laid out and do not have all the relevant information. They are designed from the supplier's perspective rather than the customer's point of view and, in general, are confusing. All invoices should include the following:

- Credit terms clearly stated
- Due date prominently displayed
- Invoice date and ship date (they should be the same)
- Items purchased explained in plain language along with relevant part numbers, including customer part numbers if required
- Quantity purchased and unit of measure as agreed with the customer
- Customer purchase order number
- Shipping data such as bill of lading number

Eliminate all information that is not needed by the customer to pay. Information that the supplier needs can be stored electronically, but the customer does not need to have access to this information. Test the new invoice format on a select group of large and small customers and your own payables department before implementing it. Involving customers in invoice design is just one way you can develop a closer relationship with them.

The information gathered in analyzing the current status of accounts receivable should be reviewed with the accounts receivable steering committee and the working capital reduction steering committee. This data will show you the major areas of operational weakness in credit and collections and probably elsewhere in the organization. If, for example, you have many claims for a defective product or a short shipment, you have issues in manufacturing and supply chain management. The analysis will show how you are touching your customers. It will also show you the complexity of your administrative processes. If you have many sets of credit terms, you can be sure that you have special pricing arrangements. The data collected and the order-to-cash map is the starting point for determining where to begin driving down accounts receivable. The approach of the team needs to be one of making it easy for the customer to pay on time. Focus on eliminating the errors causing the disputed items and meeting with the top customers to determine their invoice information requirements for making timely payments.

Have a correct customer master list

An incorrect customer master file creates many errors. Most companies I have visited do not regularly maintain their customer master list. It is imperative to routinely review all data in the customer master file. Set up a schedule similar to an inventory cycle count program. Correct the customer name, ship-to address, mail-to address, telephone number, fax number, e-mail address, billing requirements (for example, purchase order number, customer part number and unit of measure), purchasing agent name, accounts payable contact, and any other pertinent information required to properly process an order and collect should be in the customer master file. If you don't have the correct information in the customer master file you cannot possibly have an efficient accounts receivable management program. Form a team to refresh the customer master. Incorrect customer master data issues usually only surface when you perform a systems conversion. Try to catch them sooner.

Involve the sales force in the receivables improvement program

The sales force should work with the customer financial service department to set annual DSO objectives for each key customer along with a strategy to reduce DSO and/or credit terms. The customer financial services manager should frequently attend sales meetings, send monthly aging reports by customer to each salesperson, and meet regularly with sales personnel. Customer financial services and sales must form a partnership in order for receivables reduction to take place. Make accounts receivable part of a salesperson's responsibility. Base a part of the salesperson's bonus objectives on achieving specific DSO and bad-debt expense target levels. I have seen this as high as one-third of the bonus target. This can be used very effectively and garner a positive reaction from the sales team. Additionally, do not pay a commission on a sale until it is collected. I once saw a very large commission paid on a sale at the end of the year and the sale subsequently turned out to be the company's largest bad debt in years.

Focus on the top twenty customers

This sounds too simplistic a task to be included in the book. However, I can assure you that most accounts receivable management programs do not segment the customer base and focus on key customers. In most businesses the top twenty customers will generate over 80% of sales. In many cases the top ten customers account for over 90% of sales. These customers should be treated with the utmost care and attention. The following are the key elements of a top-twenty-customer program:

- **Assemble teams from sales, marketing, finance, manufacturing and logistics.** Assign them the key accounts. Make each member responsible for meeting customer requirements. This team should be the focal point for all activity with the account.

- **Have a very detailed customer specification profile list that is kept current.** Have yearly objectives for sales, profitability, DSO, credit terms, inventory turnover, on time delivery, out of stock and other pertinent measures for each customer. Make sure the objective definitions are relevant to the customer. Each member of the customer team should have annual customer objectives that are part of the compensation program.

- **Prepare an annual operating and strategic plan for each major customer**. It should include such actions as new logistics programs, new invoicing programs, and the introduction of new sales growth and early payment bonuses.

- **Have each member of the team regularly visit his/her counterpart at the customer's office or plant and work on the specific issues identified in the planning process.** Make sure the plan is reviewed with the customer before it is finalized.

This effort can be used to establish a certified customer program where quantity, quality, delivery timing, shipping packaging, invoicing requirements, payment procedures, dispute resolution procedures, price and credit terms are defined. Notice price and credit terms are listed last. You should only talk about price and terms after all the other elements of the relationship are defined. All of the elements of the product and service program impact the price and credit terms.

The sales force will not want anyone else to visit the customer but it is imperative that a visit takes place. Having finance people visit customer accounts payable personnel will reveal information about customer payment practices and requirements. It is much harder for the customer to turn down a request for payment when you have a personal relationship with him/her. The customer accounts payable personnel should explain the payment program and how the payables department is managed. You can determine what causes an invoice to be rejected and how to manage disputed items. You can also form teams to eliminate administrative errors specific to major customers. Your customer's payables department doesn't like to receive invoices with errors. It creates extra work, which adds to the cost of doing business with you.

Settle customer disputes and claims quickly

I recommend settling all customer complaints within five days of receipt. You should settle all small claims immediately, focusing on the large claims and eliminating the root causes. Many companies have large backlogs of unprocessed claims from customers. They spend an inordinate amount of time tracking and processing claims due to complicated approval procedures. They require many people to approve them and there is no timetable followed for dispute resolution. Often, the company waits for the customer to complain before settling the dispute. The credit and collections department usually is in charge of managing disputed items since the customer will not pay until the dispute is settled. This is a poor way to manage customer relations.

Disputed items are booked as an expense the moment they are received by the company. That is correct accounting policy. Having various people not approving claims because they don't want their budget to be charged is only hurting customer relations. The company already has recorded the expense.

My experience has been that at least 95% of customer claims and disputes are settled in favor of the customer. There is usually a value threshold below which 99% of all customer claims are settled in favor of the customer. For example, in one company that I consulted with, I determined that 99% of all claims of $1,000 or less were approved. The supplier decided to give the sales force automatic approval authority for claims of $1,000 or less. The sales force was required to complete a claim report for follow-up at a latter date. The customers and sales force were very pleased with the new policy.

Analyze recently settled customer claims to determine which ones were approved and which were not granted. Analyze how long it is taking to approve claims. The policy needs to be changed to automatically approve all claims below a specified level. Do not tell the customer. Establish a program to track the value and frequency of small-value claims. Focus on large claims and determine what caused them to occur in the first place. Fix the root cause of the claims. Give the automatic claim-settling authority to the sales force. They will gain stature with their customer and it will help them develop a stronger relationship with the accounts.

Make sure you have a disputed item approval policy that is easy to understand, focuses on clearing claims as quickly as possible and, most importantly, has a follow-up program to determine the root causes of the claims so they can be fixed.

Establish a credit term policy

Credit terms should be as short as possible. This is intuitively obvious but I guarantee you that no one challenges the status quo on credit terms. The shorter the credit terms, the more the customer can buy with a given credit line. Thus, keeping credit terms short allows greater sales for the same credit risk. Any credit term beyond cash-on-delivery is an extension of a loan by the supplier to the customer. Most terms are set following industry customs and standards. They should be set as short as possible for the standard terms and negotiated for all large customers. When there are errors in delivering a service or product to the customer and errors in the invoicing process, it creates reasons for the customer not to pay within stated credit terms. Making the terms of payment difficult to understand or not tailoring payment information to meet customer requirements can be reasons for the customer not to pay on time. Inflexible enforcement of credit limits and terms can also be a great source of customer dissatisfaction.

The key is to work with the sales and marketing departments to structure selling arrangements with large customers that meet their needs for quantity, quality, delivery reliability, price, credit terms and administrative activities including electronic invoicing and payment and dispute resolution. Negotiate these terms as a package with the customer. Better yet, establish a certified customer program as previously described.

The ultimate objective is to have the customer pay cash on delivery. You can make this happen in more situations than you can imagine. First, request that all small transactions be paid with a purchasing card. Some customers with many small transactions may initially resist this idea but try it anyway. Point out to the buyer the advantages of using a purchasing card for small orders. All spare part sales should be made on a purchasing card. This may sound simplistic but many companies do not tailor credit terms to make it easy for customers to pay on time.

Renegotiate credit terms with key customers

Renegotiating shorter credit terms can improve cash flow. In some cases, you may opt to offer a discount to garner shorter payment terms. The concern is that a discount doesn't necessarily guarantee that the customer will pay on time. I only advocate offering a discount if it is paid as a bonus and done in conjunction with other programs such as meeting sales targets and paying all bills on time. Keep in mind that too large a discount may prove to be uneconomical.

A golden rule of accounts receivable management is to never grant a temporary or, worse yet, a permanent increase in credit terms, even for a large customer. I have seen temporary increases in credit terms to help a customer in financial difficulty become permanent. If fact, I have never seen a customer return to shorter credit terms without a financial inducement. If a major customer requests financial assistance, do not agree to longer credit terms. You can negotiate a special discount for a specific period of time but do not agree to longer terms. Changes in price can be renegotiated but credit terms tend to be untouchable in most cases unless they are packaged with the annual negotiations. The worst discussion I ever had with a customer involved getting him back to original credit terms after granting extended terms for a limited time. It was a very ugly conversation.

The key to changing the payment practices and credit terms of large customers is to develop customer partnership programs. The programs are developed by sales, finance and operations to make it easier for the customer to do business with you. As previously discussed, these programs should be targeted for specific customers during the annual planning process by the customer teams.

Some examples of value-added programs are:

- **An early payment discount linked with a volume rebate incentive**
  The rebate is paid only if the customer pays all invoices on time and meets the sales increase objective.

- **Including a early payment discount with a logistics program to improve customer receiving time**
  Pay the early payment discount as a rebate at the end of the year if the customer pays all invoices during the year on time.

- **Linking a discount to early payment combined with an improved administrative program**
  For example, for a customer receiving many invoices each week, change the invoicing to weekly batch invoicing with weekly terms such as 15 days end-of-week. The end-of-week terms can be adjusted to coincide with the timing of the customer's payment processing.

You can also combine logistics and administrative improvement programs and reduce the customer's costs and working capital while at the same time reducing your costs and working capital.

In any discount program you need to carefully consider your full cost of capital and not offer any discounts that are uneconomical. You also need to understand the customer's cost of capital and if the customer even considers cost of capital when determining whether to accept discounts for shorter credit terms. For example, if the customer's purchasing agent is measured only on net cost and is not responsible for working capital, he will be receptive to discount programs.

In one program I was involved with, a supplier was able to introduce a 1.5% discount for electronic payment on delivery for a very large customer with a maximum of 30 days to resolve disputes. The terms were part of a large contract for a new product. Originally the supplier was going to offer standard 30-day net terms. The customer had advised that his policy was to pay in 45 days. In fact, the DSO for the program was more likely to be 55 days. In programs of this nature there would be significant write-offs of receivables over 90 days past due involving disputes that were never fully resolved. The customer accepted the payment on delivery terms and actually paid each invoice on delivery. The supplier never had a receivable. In fact, the supplier consistently owed the customer for claims such as defective products and short shipment. By eliminating the receivable, the supplier eliminated a major asset and source of continuing issues on collection from a large and important customer.

In the example, if annual sales were $10,000,000, the average receivable avoided, assuming DSO of 55, would be approximately $1,500,000. The after-tax discount on the annual sales, assuming a 40% tax rate, is .9% or $90,000. Assuming the cost of capital is 10%, eliminating the receivable increased the economic value $150,000. Thus, the total program created net economic value of $60,000 and significantly reduced bad debt risks. This does not take into account the complete elimination of a major problem in the relationship with the customer concerning paying within terms and the cost savings from having to settle old disputed items that may not be valid. These issues can become very onerous depending on the product and complexity of the transactions with the customer. Except for the numbers used, this is an actual example and it worked extremely well. You can use the same methodology to determine whether or not to accept a supplier discount for early payment.

Establish a credit line policy

Establishing credit lines is an art that many try to make a science. The key is to grant enough credit to customers so they can operate their business yet pay invoices within credit terms. With longer the credit terms, fewer orders can be accepted since you will reach the customer's credit limit even though the customer still needs product. There is a trade-off between terms and amount of credit the customer needs.

When establishing a credit line policy first examine the customer base and determine annual sales by customer and average order size. The top twenty customers may have very different credit needs from the rest of the customer group. Focus your effort on extending credit to the top twenty customers and automatically grant credit of one to two months' sales to all other customers assuming they are small (less than 2% of annual sales) relative to the total annual sales of the company, have no history of bankruptcy, have a good record of paying within stated credit terms and have been in business over one year. Follow the credit enforcement policy and hold orders if the policy is violated. Putting most small customers on payment with a purchasing card avoids credit line, collection and bad debt issues.

My approach to credit-granting for large customers is the following:

- **Determine the credit history and financial strength of the customer from a credit rating agency, other suppliers and/or a bank**. Ask the customer for financial statements and analyze them. If the customer has a history of slow pay or has a weak financial condition, offer purchasing card terms. As a last resort request payment in advance.

- **Determine how long the customer has been in business and if his company has any bankruptcy history.** Any company in business more than one year is usually a good credit risk. If the customer has a bankruptcy or has been in business less than one year, ask for purchasing card payment or cash in advance.

- **Set credit limits reflecting the customer's ability to pay and purchasing requirements.** Many companies use fixed formulas published by credit rating agencies to set credit limits. I have seen this approach used to set ridiculously low credit limits for major credit-worthy companies. Avoid this approach for them. However, you should apply some judgment in granting credit to your major customers. Develop a risk/reward calculation that sets credit limits based on the amount the customer will buy and the profitability of the account. Assuming the customer has been in business over one year, has no bankruptcy history, is financially strong and has a record of paying no more than 30 days late, you should grant credit. The amount of credit granted should be related to how much the customer will buy and the profitability of the business.

The first step is to determine how much the customer will buy in a one-year period. Also determine the gross profit margin on the business. Set the maximum amount of credit granted at any time equal to 50% of the forecasted annual gross profit. With this approach the risk/reward ratio will be 50% over any one-year period. The actual credit line should probably be only twice the average monthly purchase amount unless there is seasonality in the buying pattern. For example, if the customer is going to buy $10,000 per month and terms are 30 days, the credit line should be $22,000. You need a 10% override to allow for sales variation patterns. If the annual sales will be $120,000 and the gross margin is 40%, the maximum you can extend and at least recover cost of production in six months is $24,000. This quick analysis gives you an estimate of the risk of loss and potential profitability. In this example, you shouldn't grant terms above 30 days and you don't want to grant a credit line of more than $24,000. If the business grows and the customer pays on time, you can increase the credit line but only after performing the risk/reward analysis. I have used this credit-limit-setting approach very successfully.

Develop a credit-granting system that is easy and flexible that allows the business to operate without cumbersome rules. Remember, the customer is your friend and the only reason you stay in business is because you have customers.

You can use credit-rating agency systems to develop credit lines but I find the easiest way to set credit lines for your large customers is to use the technique described in this chapter. You always want to relate the credit line to the customer's intended purchases and the profitability of the account.

Credit departments are often very tight on granting credit. Most of their effort is spent on establishing rigid credit limits. Focus on granting credit sufficient for the customer to do business with you and then make sure it is easy for the customer to pay on time. Make it very clear up front with the sales force and the customer that invoices are to be paid on time. If you have concerns about the customer's ability or intent to pay in a timely manner, make the customer pay with a purchasing card or pay in advance. The one caveat is international sales. Unless you have established a strong relationship with an international customer, ask for payment in advance either with cash or a purchasing card. Otherwise, ask for a confirmed, irrevocable letter of credit.

Set fair credit and collection rules and follow them

You need a clear policy on collecting accounts receivable. Credit granting and settling claims have already been discussed. I suggest the following collection rules:

- **Follow up on past-due invoices within three days of being past due.** The faster you follow up, the faster any open issues will be resolved. In some cases you may wish to call one week in advance of a large invoice due date to ensure the order is satisfactory and payment will be made on time.

- **Stop shipment on all new orders if the customer is past due 10 days after promising to pay and there is no disputed item**. Always inform the salesperson and the customer before holding a shipment. Make sure you offer the customer the chance to pay past-due invoices with a purchasing card or electronically.

- **Send all customers to collection if the invoice is 60 days past due, there is no promise to pay and there is no disputed item.** Always inform the sales force before taking the action. The customer also has to be informed before sending him to collection. Document this action with a letter advising that you will send the customer to collection if no payment is made within a certain period of time. A lawyer should draft the sample letter to make sure you have covered all the legal issues. Always make one last request to have payment made electronically or with a purchasing card.

These rules assume the customer buys regularly from you. If the customer only buys periodically you need to have good records and flag any accounts that paid late on previous purchases. At order entry, tell the late payers to be prompt on the current order or risk being placed on cash-in-advance or purchasing card payment status.

Communication with the sales force and the customer on your collection policy is vital. Everyone needs to understand the rules. Make sure the sales force has reviewed and understands the credit-granting rules and collection policy. Tell the customer that you expect to be paid on time, which means the payment must be received on the due date. Credit card companies make this very clear.

Chargeback for unauthorized deductions

All unauthorized deductions should be charged back to the customer. This includes unearned discounts. Have a program in place to track unauthorized deductions by customer and the type of deduction. Design a process to follow up on the reasons for the deductions and take action to ensure they do not occur in the future. If a customer continually takes unauthorized deductions for invalid reasons, you need to place him/her on payment-in-advance either with cash or a on a purchasing card.

Charging interest on past-due balances

There are arguments for and against charging interest on past-due balances. In some industries it is accepted practice to charge interest on past-due account balances. However, this is not always the case. If you charge interest on past-due balances, you need to have a very clear and concise policy that is easily explained to all involved, including the sales force, customers, customer financial services department and customer sales representatives. Charge a fair and reasonable rate of interest on balances that are clearly past due. Do not violate usury laws. Make certain that the calculation procedure is clearly understood and consistently applied.

Charging interest on past-due balances can be fraught with risk if it is not the norm in your industry and/or you have poor processes with many product and shipping defects and administrative errors.

Automate the collection process to the extent possible

Implement a purchasing card program as soon as possible and instruct order entry personnel to ask for payment by purchasing card for all small orders. As discussed above, you will need to define a small order and/or a small customer. The purchasing card program must be integrated with the existing accounting system. Otherwise you will just create more accounting work and introduce the possibility for more errors.

Work with large customers to implement electronic payment with associated payment data. They should want to do this since it will save them time and help them with forecasting cash flow. With the introduction of new check-clearing rules there is no more bank check float so the reason to pay by check has been eliminated. When you and your customers automate payment processes, fewer errors will occur and costs will decrease for both parties. Link automated payment with certified shipment programs. Introduce shorter payment terms with any improved logistics or administrative program.

If you can have your large customers on a certified shipping program with electronic invoicing and payment and small customers paying with purchasing cards, the administrative work in credit and collections and accounts receivable accounting will be virtually eliminated.

Check all orders at order entry

All orders should be checked at order entry to make sure the customer is within the credit limit, including the new order, and has no past-due invoices without a valid dispute. If either condition occurs, place the order on hold. If the credit line will be exceeded, determine if a higher credit line is possible. If not, contact the sales person and explain that the customer will exceed the credit limit and the order cannot be fulfilled without a payment on current invoices outstanding. In the case of past-due invoices the customer should be contacted and asked to pay the past-due invoices so the new order can be processed. If the customer cannot and/or will not pay the past due invoices, contact the sales person. It is important to keep communication open between the customer service order entry team, the customer and the sales person.

Prepare a credit and collections policy and procedures manual

Document the various policies and procedures you have established for the function. Use this as a training aid for new sales and customer financial services people. Make sure the manual is easy to read and not too long. No one will use it if it is cumbersome.

Train the sales force and customer financial services team

Your sales force needs to be trained to present the credit policy to customers and to work with the customer financial services department to quickly resolve customer disputes. You also need to train the customer financial services department on department policies and on how to handle collection calls. Develop standard responses for the major excuses and valid reasons customers will not pay on time. Automate sending invoices and proof of delivery with e-mail and faxing. If the customer is past due, offer purchasing card payment or electronic funds transfer.

Summary

Changes in accounts receivable management cannot be made overnight. It is important to get started and then make changes incrementally. Start by forming the team, doing the analysis and working on resolving the main reasons customers do not pay on time. Implement a significant training program. The result will be improved customer service, reduced DSO and a reduction in the absolute level of accounts receivable, giving rise to improved cash flow. Your first step may be as simple as developing a new invoice. The entire focus and purpose of the accounts receivable management improvement program is to make it easy for customers to pay quickly. Never lose sight of that objective.

Chapter 11

INVENTORY MANAGEMENT

Excellent inventory management is the key to reducing working capital

If you take the necessary steps to drive down inventory you will have also done much of the work necessary to drive down accounts receivable and manage accounts payable. Reducing inventory requires fast, flexible, defect-free production and on-time delivery of the right product to the customer. It also requires excellent customer and supplier relations. Achieving this level of operational excellence will make it easier for customers to pay quickly. It will also allow for supplier credit terms to be renegotiated. In the study of fifteen manufacturing companies, inventory turnover was 5.6. This means that on average these companies had about 2.1 months of inventory on hand. In general, they all had significant levels of raw materials, some work in progress and significant finished goods inventory. On average, the companies had 3.7 weeks of sales in finished goods. This is an extremely high level of finished goods inventory for companies with little or no seasonality or aging requirements.

Reducing inventory is important

Most companies turn inventory four to six times a year, which means inventory turns once every two to two three months. If you have $1.5 million in inventory and it turns four times per year, you can reduce inventory by $1,000,000 by increasing turnover to once a month, or twelve times a year. Unless you have a product that needs to age before selling, such as wine or cheese, or a seasonal product, you should be able to manage inventory turnover of once a month. Increasing inventory turnover to twenty-four times a year from twelve doesn't drive down the value of inventory very much. However, by lowering inventory to that level, process issues that can reduce customer service and product quality are exposed. Inventory is a buffer for process errors. The lower your inventory level, the fewer process errors you can tolerate and still provide outstanding customer service.

The objective should be to expeditiously manufacture what you sell

I have seen businesses manufacture and ship the product to customers on the same day in a number of operations, from stock products to custom manufacturing. Most of the raw materials in these operations came in and the finished goods went out in a 24-hour period. I have observed inventory turnover in a custom manufacturing plant as high as 100. Most people do not feel this is possible but it can be achieved without increasing costs. In fact, the lower the inventory or, conversely, the higher the inventory turnover, the lower the manufacturing cost. I do not advocate trying to achieve inventory turnover of 100, but you can achieve inventory turnover of 12 by turning inventory once a month.

Outstanding operations execution is the key to working capital reduction

Driving down inventory requires achieving outstanding operations execution. Strong operations execution must be a major component of any business strategy. The best product and marketing strategy will fail without outstanding operating execution. It separates the good from the great companies. These techniques can also be used in operations in a variety of industries, such as insurance companies and hospitals.

Inventory loses value over time

I once heard a consultant call warehouses inventory aging rooms. He was right on the mark. The longer you hold an item in inventory, the more likely it is to diminish in value for many reasons. Items in inventory can become:

- Obsolete
- Soiled
- Damaged
- Lost
- Stolen

All of these result in reduced value of the inventory. The best possible result that can happen to inventory is that it is used in production or sold and shipped. The longer items remain in inventory, the more likely they are to become a write-off because they are not usable for one of the above reasons. Managing the risk of loss of inventory requires considerable time, effort and cost.

Holding inventory increases expenses

In addition to the cost of risk of loss discussed above, inventory storage creates significant expenses for:

- Insurance
- Personnel (to move, count and safeguard)
- Warehouse space (rent or depreciation)
- Warehouse equipment
- Utilities

Minimizing inventory can significantly reduce costs and thereby improve a company's cash flow, EBIT, return on investment and economic value. The cost to manage and operate an efficient warehouse is expensive. Do not underestimate the cost and effort required to effectively manage a warehouse operation.

Slow inventory turnover reduces the ability to correct production errors

If you produce finished goods that are defective and do not ship them until two or three months after production, it is almost impossible to trace the source of the defect. No one will remember what happened even if you have excellent production records. Memories fade with time. It will be difficult to go back to a supplier and discuss a faulty raw material three or four months after receipt. The personnel involved may have changed during the time between production and detection of the defect. If you produce a product today from raw materials delivered within the last week and ship it within a week of manufacturing, it is much easier to determine the source of any product defect.

An example of poor inventory management

I have had first-hand experience in managing inventory in a warehouse. During the summer before I entered college I worked in a warehouse that was filled to the rafters with product. The aisles were narrow and it was very difficult to maneuver the lift trucks. As they tried to maneuver through the aisles, the lift truck drivers repeatedly damaged material loaded on pallets. Since the owner of the warehouse berated the workers when they damaged materials, the foreman moved all damaged goods to a separate pallet. At the end of the shift the damaged goods were stored in a back corner of the warehouse. The owner never paid attention to an inventory count and the workers avoided showing him the pallet with damaged goods, so he didn't realized that damaged goods were counted as part of the inventory. If he had initiated a more robust inventory management system that included an orderly warehouse, he would have had fewer damaged goods and would have avoided all the effort to manage an overly large volume of inventory. I am sure similar situations are repeated countless times in warehouses all over the world. It doesn't have to happen.

Holding inventory does not guarantee meeting customer needs

The finished goods inventory you hold may not necessarily be the right product to meet a customer's order. Additionally, you may not have the correct raw material to manufacture what has been sold. What the customer buys may not be what you have in inventory and the customer order ends up in a backlog. You then have to purchase new raw materials to meet the customer demand. Meanwhile, the old inventory remains in a warehouse waiting to be a write-off while incurring storage and management expenses. There is nothing more frustrating to a customer than having an order placed in a backlog.

Keys to reducing inventory

In order to minimize inventory you need to have:

- Clean, safe and efficient facilities
- A close link to key customers' demand requirements
- Efficient communications with primary suppliers on your demand forecast
- Very fast and on-time delivery of defect-free raw materials and parts from suppliers
- Error-free, fast, and flexible manufacturing
- Fast, on-time error-free delivery of orders to customers

Achieving success in these six areas should not be difficult if you have commitment from the organization, particularly operations management. If your operations management team does not buy into the program, you must bring them on board before any meaningful work can be done. Old thinking will not work. Desktop and mobile computing and improved telecommunications have changed the world of operations. The Internet can now be used extensively to speed manufacturing. Most of the materials ordering and scheduling that once was done in an office can now be done on the shop floor via fax or e-mail by the people running the plant. Having a highly clean, efficient plant with zero injuries run by empowered people on the factory floor is the only way to achieve operations excellence and minimize working capital.

Action steps to reduce inventory

- Appoint a leader and leadership team.
- Develop a communication and training program.
- Tour all of the facilities including the interior, exterior and grounds.
- Review the safety record and injury costs.
- Define operating performance measures.
- Review the backlog over the past year.
- Review the disputed item list.
- Analyze inventory turnover.
- Analyze purchases and suppliers of the top twenty raw materials.
- Analyze sales of the top twenty products and customers.
- Analyze product design for simplification opportunities.
- Analyze the order-to-shipment cycle.
- Begin a manufacturing excellence program.

Once the analysis has been completed you will have a clear picture of where you can take time and defects out of the manufacturing process. The popular term for the type of manufacturing program you need is lean manufacturing. There are numerous articles and books written about this approach to managing a factory. You do not have to do all of the above at once. Form the team, take a tour of the facilities and review the safety record. Also review the disputed item list and backlog list and analyze inventory turnover. These actions will tell you the critical issues to attack first.

Appoint a leader and leadership team

The inventory reduction team leader has to be the head of operations. The leadership team should include people from manufacturing, finance, logistics, materials management, human resources and purchasing. This team's members need to be very change-oriented. They do not have to be the head of their respective areas but it is imperative that they be viewed as leaders by the rest of the organization. The human resources person must be in charge of training and communications. If a union is involved, make sure the union leadership is included in planning and implementation. The union must see how the program will benefit its members. This cannot be a people-reduction program. Safer working conditions in a better work environment are key selling points. If there are inventory management changes, the finance person will have to make sure that the accounting is done properly. The finance team will want to link the inventory management program and purchasing changes with the accounts payable improvement program. The logistics and materials management team may have to install new demand forecasting and materials handling systems. The purchasing team will have to redefine their purchasing program.

The people on the inventory team will probably overlap with the accounts payable team. The two teams should not work independently. Their activity must be coordinated to make sure that any changes to various policies are consistent. Changes in supplier relations dictated by the inventory program need to be coordinated with all supplier relations changes from the accounts payable improvement program. This sounds logical but you will need to make sure there is a process to manage this activity. The steering committee is probably the best place to ensure that adequate coordination between teams is taking place.

Develop a communication and training program

The human resources person should be responsible for developing the training program and possibly the communications effort. In large companies there will be a separate department to handle the communications program. Employees need to know why changes are being made, what is expected of them and what it will do for them. People don't like change unless you can convince them that it will positively impact them. I once heard a CEO remark that he liked change but only when he was in charge of it. Involving the workforce in developing the workplace changes helps obtain buy-in. Installing comprehensive training and communications programs is crucial to the success of the inventory reduction program. To achieve very high levels of inventory turnover, fundamental changes must be made in the way production is managed. Move in a step-by-step manner to make changes in the way the factory and warehouse operations are run.

Additionally, the human resources person should review the compensation system to determine if changes should be made in pay practices to reward workers for achieving certain knowledge levels or performance targets. Fair pay for performance programs gets the full attention of the work force. Employees will work hard to meet the targets. The key is to set reasonable targets on important performance measures. If a union is involved you may find it difficult to change your compensation program.

Tour the facilities including the interior and exterior and grounds

Once the team is formed, have members take a detailed tour of all facilities. This may have to be done in several sessions to fully cover warehouses and plants. Tours should include the interior, exterior and grounds of each facility. Include people from every facility to take notes of possible changes. Have a checklist of items to review at each facility. You will be amazed at the issues you will find.

- Inadequate housekeeping
- Scrap being stored in the plant and warehouse
- Unsafe working conditions
- Unclean locker rooms, restrooms and canteens
- Inadequate security
- Dirty floors, walls and ceilings
- Inadequate lighting
- Insufficient maintenance
- Inefficient materials flow
- Inefficient machine layout
- Significant work-in-process inventory

I have toured plants all over the world that produce many different types of products ranging from food to machinery. The primary difference in the condition of the plants was the management team's commitment to excellence. I have seen wonderful plants in newly developing countries and awful plants in developed countries. The attitude of the management team in the plants made all the difference.

Tour the inside and outside of all facilities, including the entrance, parking lot, and shipping and receiving areas. Make sure there is a secure, sufficiently lighted, adequate parking area and a secure entrance to the facility. You cannot expect high performance from employees working in poorly lighted, dirty, and unsafe workspaces. You also cannot expect them to want to perform if their locker rooms, restrooms and canteen are not well maintained. Start the program by cleaning the plant and warehouse and instituting good housekeeping and safety practices.

Be careful when disposing of scrap in the plant. Make sure you have properly recorded it as scrap and it is not included in inventory. I worked on an audit in a plant where the new manager had cleaned the plant by removing all scrap. During the year-end audit, he discovered that the scrap had been recorded in the books as inventory. When he threw it out, he tossed all the profit for the year. This doesn't mean you should not clean a plant, but it does mean you need to make sure the accounting for scrap and inventory is done properly.

Work on improving housekeeping and safety and make sure the employees have attractive and well-maintained locker rooms, restrooms and canteen facilities. They will know you are serious about making fundamental change if the facilities look attractive and are safe. You have to walk the walk and talk the talk. Making positive improvements in working conditions will show workers that you are serious about making significant change in operations.

Analyze the safety record and injury costs

If you don't already have one, form a safety team. Investigate every injury and determine how each could have been avoided. Review the injury record over the past year. This should be the first concern of the inventory reduction team. Also review the workers' compensation costs, number of lost time injuries and average time to return to work after an injury. You should analyze injuries by type of injury and accident. If you have a high injury rate, you will want to initiate a safety program to reduce the recordable injury rate below 1. Your workers' compensation insurer or broker should be able to provide a specialist in developing safety programs. The insurer or broker should also be able to assist in developing injury management programs, including return-to-work programs for lost time injuries. Having a safe workplace is critical to achieving operating excellence. A high injury rate is usually indicative of other manufacturing problems such a poor product quality and slow production speed.

Do not tolerate unsafe acts in your facilities by anyone, including visitors. Contractors were responsible for two of the worst accidents in companies where I worked. Both contractor-related accidents resulted in deaths. Place a bulletin board area near the employees' locker room or canteen to display the safety program results against target. Tailor the safety performance measures to meet your specific business. Make the safety performance results visible to employees and discuss them in employee meetings.

Developing a strong safety program requires intense focus from the organization. It can be done in parallel with other improvement programs. However, you have to stress to the workforce that safety is the most important part of their job. Otherwise you will not achieve your safety improvement targets. A zero recordable injury rate is achievable in manufacturing but it takes strong management commitment.

Define operating measures

Once the team is formed you will need to define operating measures of success. I propose that, at a minimum, you have the following measures:

- **Order-to-delivery time per order for custom and stock products**
  Set targets and then investigate how to reduce the time.

- **On-time delivery to customers**
  This is a critical measure of customer service. You must meet promises to customers for delivery reliability. The measure should be reviewed with the customer to make sure you are defining delivery reliability in the same terms as the customer.

- **Product defects per 100,000 units**
  Define how to measure a product defect. Talk with your customers about what is an acceptable product quality and use that definition to help define product defects.

- **Shipping defects per 100,000 shipments**
  Define how to measure a shipping defect. Discuss with customers what is acceptable delivery quality and what causes defects.

- **Recordable injury rate**
  Target zero injuries. You cannot have a productive operation if people are being hurt on the job. Any recordable injury rate over 0 is unacceptable. If your injury rate is over 3, you have a huge problem. Place a continual emphasis on safety.

Review the backlog over the past year

The backlog will tell you which products you were unable to ship as ordered. Develop a list of the causes of the backlog and develop programs to eliminate them. In some businesses, such as construction or long-term contract manufacturing programs, having a production backlog is part of the business practice. However, in most businesses a backlog means that a customer's delivery requirement is not being met.

Review the disputed item list

This list should show which product quality and delivery issues to pursue. Damaged goods, short shipment and product defects must be eliminated. This is very important. The customer is telling you what is wrong in very clear terms. The customer is probably not paying the invoice because there is a problem with the order. Make fixing these issues a very high priority. It never ceases to amaze me that the same disputed item issues continue to occur year after year and no one takes the responsibility to fix them. Simply laying out a pallet more efficiently and providing better packaging can, in many cases, eliminate damaged goods and short shipment issues. Determine what is causing the problem and then take action to fix it. Many times it will require visiting the customer to discover the root causes of the problem. Resolving disputed item root causes requires close teamwork and strong customer and supplier relations. Make disputed item root causes the next item on the steering committee agenda after making sure you have a strong safety program and a clean, well organized plant. These issues can be worked on in parallel.

Analyze inventory turnover

You may have to take a physical inventory just to find out what you have on hand. You will have raw materials and parts, work in process and finished goods inventory. Analyze each aspect of inventory to determine turnover rates by type of inventory. If you have been having significant inventory write-offs, take a physical inventory at least quarterly. Segregate raw material inventory into categories depending on value and turnover. High-value and high-turnover raw materials and parts need to be ordered and delivered frequently as needed. In a cellular manufacturing operation the ordering is managed from the shop floor through e-mail or fax. In most operations the high-value, high-usage materials and parts are received every day and in some cases every hour. They are moved directly to the manufacturing operation and never stored in a warehouse. The high-value, high-sales products are produced and shipped every day. There should be virtually no work in process if the manufacturing line is balanced and sequentially includes all steps to produce and ship a product. In some cases you may want some work in process instead of maintaining any finished goods. Work can be completed and the product shipped immediately after any final testing. Avoid large pools of raw materials, significant work in process between each manufacturing process and weeks of possible demand in finished goods inventory.

Analyze the trade-offs between quantity discounts, transportation costs and storage expenses when determining the economic order size. The key point is to analyze the main raw materials in terms of value and usage and determine how frequently they should be ordered and delivered.

Small changes in materials specifications can make a significant difference in the amount and frequency of ordering. For example, instead of having shipping containers pre-printed with information, have required information contained on a label that can be applied to a standard package. In general, labels are inexpensive and can be changed easily. Standard packaging materials can be ordered in smaller quantities than pre-printed packages.

I have ignored seasonality in the discussion. This is an issue that needs to be dealt with on a customer-by-customer, product-by-product basis. In some cases, such as food manufacturing or holiday demand, you may not be able to significantly reduce seasonal inventory. However, having flexible, fast and error-free manufacturing facilities will allow you to produce your product closer to the anticipated shipping date. It will also allow you to more easily meet demand changes during the season.

Analyze the top twenty raw materials and parts

From the inventory turnover analysis, you will be able to identify the top twenty raw materials and parts. Focus your energy on managing these raw materials and parts and suppliers. Senior management should focus on negotiating the contracts for these products. The shop floor should be given responsibility for controlling the ordering of the materials based on production requirements. This is a critical part of the inventory reduction process.

Analyze the top twenty suppliers

This information can also be useful in the accounts payable management program. Data can be obtained from the accounts payable and/or purchasing records. Combining the top suppliers and materials and parts data will give you a profile of the most important suppliers.

Develop supplier certification programs for quality and service and require all key suppliers to become certified. Start taking delivery daily or as often as needed within hours of placing the order. These requests should be part of the program to negotiate quantity, quality, delivery time, price, credit terms, method of payment and dispute resolution procedures with the major suppliers. This is where coordination between finance, operations, materials management, logistics and purchasing is critical. Develop specifications by material and supplier and design a supplier negotiating strategy based on requirements.

One part of the supplier management process is to determine if the number of suppliers can be reduced. You should not have more than one major supplier for each raw material and part. It is a good idea, however, to have a qualified second source as an emergency backup for all critical materials and parts.

In many inventory management programs, the supply chain and purchasing personnel try to force suppliers to maintain large inventories in warehouses near the customer plant or, worse yet, in your plant or warehouse. This does not guarantee that the right product will be delivered on time and be defect-free. The supplier must move toward a just-in-time manufacturing and supply program to effectively meet inventory management requirements.

Analyze the top twenty customers and products

This information will be available from your accounts receivable program. Begin a program of working with the top customers to receive demand and inventory level data. This information is necessary to plan daily production. Your objective should be to manufacture and ship what you sell each day. In order to accomplish fast changes in production you will need to have very fast, defect-free and flexible production facilities. There are demand-forecasting programs available to assist you in developing production schedules. Achieving good demand forecasting information is critical in designing an inventory management program. It drives production scheduling and raw materials ordering. Share your production forecast with key raw material suppliers. This activity, linked with defect-free, fast and flexible manufacturing, will drive inventory to very low levels.

Review product design for simplification

Examine the top twenty products you sell to determine if they use common raw materials and parts. Determine if the design can be simplified from a production point of view. Inventory management is easier with fewer materials and parts. This is a very important step in trying to simplify production. Minimizing the number of raw materials and parts used in production will greatly simplify inventory management. Use standard raw materials and parts whenever possible. Custom parts and specialized raw materials create order size and timing issues. Challenge over-engineered solutions that require non-standard parts and raw materials. However, be careful not to diminish product uniqueness or functionality in any redesign.

Analyze the order-to-shipment cycle

If you have not already done so in the value chain analysis, review the order-to-shipment processes. Look for opportunities to take time, defects, variation and non-value-added work out of the order-to-shipment cycle. Any delays in processing are unacceptable. The only valid reason to hold an order is when the customer is past due in paying for previous shipments and there are no unresolved disputed items. You do not want backlogs of orders unless they are for non-stock products. It is important to make sure you can meet promised delivery dates for all orders.

Begin a manufacturing excellence program

There are many books written on the subject of manufacturing excellence. I will present only a very small summary of the issues you must manage to develop a robust manufacturing program. As stated many times before, you need fast, error-free and flexible manufacturing in order to significantly reduce inventory. Reduce set-up time and take defects and variation out of the manufacturing process while continuing to increase production speed. Video all setup operations and then review the video with the setup team. Look for opportunities to reduce in-line setup time with off-line setup of equipment and materials and create better tool layout. If a customer orders product, you should be able to make and ship it in less than 48 hours. That action requires very fast set-up time, quick delivery of raw materials, and fast and error-free production. Achieving this is not easy. It takes a strong team effort to change the way a company manufactures products.

Many companies have installed a cellular manufacturing program to promote efficiency. Allocate to one team all the functions necessary to produce and ship a product. Make the team responsible for:

- Production scheduling
- Production
- Raw material ordering
- Inventory management
- Preventative maintenance
- Shipping
- Housekeeping
- Training

Pay employees for work knowledge and skill levels. I have seen many different types of manufacturing plants converted to cellular manufacturing and it worked even in highly unionized facilities. Communication with the workers throughout the process coupled with a significant amount of training is essential.

Reorganizing manufacturing operations and processes can be challenging. Do it in discrete steps. The first part of the process is to make sure the facilities are well lighted and walls, ceilings and floors are painted. Also, installing a strong safety program and good housekeeping practices must be done before you can make meaningful progress in reorganizing production.

The cellular manufacturing program can be used to segregate product manufacturing. I have seen a limited number of high-volume, long production-run products manufactured in one cell while numerous small quantity products were produced in another cell. Export products were produced in a third cell. In the high-volume production cell, process speed was critical. In the small volume, large number of products cell, quick changeover was critical. The export cell required making sure similar products had different packaging and shipping containers depending on the country where they were being shipped. In all cases the cells were responsible for the same basic activities, including raw material ordering and production scheduling.

Summary

The actions and tasks for improving inventory management discussed in this chapter are similar in complexity to the accounts receivable management program. Start by taking small steps. Operational excellence is critical to success. A tour of all your facilities, a review of the disputed item and backlog lists, a review of the injury rate and completing the inventory turnover analysis will start you on the path to significantly reducing inventory. If you have good housekeeping, well-maintained facilities and a very low injury rate and utilize the steps outlined in this chapter, you are on your way to achieving high inventory turnover and very satisfied customers, suppliers and, most importantly, loyal and happy employees. This will translate into increased cash flow and reduced financing requirements.

Chapter 12

OTHER CURRENT ASSETS

Other current assets average 2.5% of sales and range from 1% to 5% of sales. While this is not a major amount, these accounts should be managed. I recommend that a finance person oversee these accounts and determines how much can be eliminated. In a company with $10 million sales, 2.5% of sales is $250,000. I believe that money should be invested in growing the business rather than in utility and sales tax deposits.

Other receivables

Other receivables usually range from 1% to 2% of sales. This is not a big item and is usually overlooked when managing working capital. However, in a company with $10 million in sales, you have $100,000 to $200,000 invested in items for which you either paid cash or made an advance. No return on the investment is being earned. You need to earn $10,000 to $20,000 of net income in the business just to cover the cost of capital and avoid destroying wealth. Examine each item in other receivables and determine if it can be eliminated.

A finance person needs to be responsible for this account and have targets as a percentage of sales. Cutting several small current asset accounts such as prepaid expenses and other receivables can, in total, have a major impact on working capital. Don't ignore the smaller components of working capital.

Items which may be in other receivables are:

- Value added tax (VAT) refund
- Sales tax deposit

- Loans to employees
- Short-term notes receivable
- Utility deposits

VAT refunds can usually be obtained quickly if a bank guarantee is substituted for the refund. The VAT officials keep the refund as a deposit against payment of VAT owed to the government entity. The same is true for sales tax deposits.

A bank should provide loans to employees. For good corporate governance, loans or guarantee loans should not be extended to employees. In some cases, depending on the employee's position, company loans or guarantees may be illegal.

Short-term notes receivable usually are the result of business transactions such as asset sales and loans to suppliers, customers or partners. Avoid any loans to customers, suppliers or partners to the absolute extent possible. If you are going to be that deeply involved with these companies or individuals, attempt to guarantee bank loans. Do not make loans directly. They can quickly turn into an equity investment. If you do have to make a loan or a bank guarantee, always try to include a very generous equity conversion feature up front or have some other form of security.

Prepaid Expenses

Prepaid expenses usually are 1% to 2% of sales. While this is not a large item it should be managed. Using the example in the other receivables section, when sales are $10 million and prepaid expenses are 1 % to 2% of sales, the account will have $100,000 to $200,000 of items in it which were paid in advance of when they will be used. This investment is not creating value. Always question the reason for having any prepaid expenses.

Prepaid expenses may include:

- Prepaid insurance
- Deposits for conventions
- Prepaid travel expenses

A finance person should be assigned to investigate the reason for all prepaid expenses and determine how to eliminate them. For prepaid insurance, negotiate monthly premium payments or issue a bank guarantee to the insurance company. The key is to review the reason for each prepaid expense and develop a way to eliminate the need for the cash prepayment.

Assign someone the responsibility of managing these accounts. That person needs objectives and accountability.

Chapter 13

CURRENT LIABILITY MANAGEMENT

Non-interest-bearing current liabilities average about 11% and vary between 6% and 15% of sales. While current liabilities are usually half the size of current assets, they can be increased while current assets are being decreased. Accounts payable and accrued payroll and employee benefits can be managed.

Managing accounts payable is usually done by not paying a bill on time. Do not try to pay invoices late to increase current liabilities. You don't want to incur supplier ill will. You need these people. Utilities and many other items must be paid on time or a critical service will be eliminated. Determine the latest time you can pay the bill. Many bills get paid early simply because it is convenient for the payer and the actual due date is ignored. You can manage current liabilities and still achieve supplier good will. The key is to develop a management program. While this sounds very easy, many companies do not review the accounts or, if they do, the review is done by accountants and never reviewed with operating management.

You have to pay your employees on time. It is the law. Try to pay employees only twice a month. You will need input from human resources and legal advice on this issue. If you have a union you will have to review the contract. Pay retirement plans and health plans on time. However, make sure you do not pay any of them early.

Income taxes payable is not included in my definition of operating working capital but it also can be managed. Don't pay taxes early. Estimated tax payments are judgments based on forecasted profits for the full year. You need good input from operations before deciding on these payments. Ask the tax department to explain why and when you must pay taxes.

Chapter 14

ACCOUNTS PAYABLE MANAGEMENT

The objective is to have the maximum economic credit terms from suppliers

Accounts payable averaged about 7.7% of sales and ranged from 3.4% to 11.6% of sales in my study. Accounts payable can be managed. The accounts payable objective should be to have the maximum economic credit terms possible from suppliers. This sounds intuitively obvious but many companies do not negotiate credit terms with suppliers. The purchasing team usually focuses on price, which is how it is measured for compensation purposes. Supplier credit terms should be equal to or greater than credit terms granted to customers. Hopefully, you will be able to have customer credit terms substantially shorter than supplier credit terms. In theory, DPO should never be less than DSO. Given the different factors used in computing these two numbers, DPO will probably always be less than DSO.

Accounts payable management should be the easiest part of managing working capital. However, payables management is usually viewed as a financial issue and not as part of the purchasing function's responsibility. Surprisingly, even with payables averaging about 8% of sales and ranging from about 3% to 12% of sales, many companies are not organized to effectively manage them. The payables management process, if any, usually only involves not paying invoices on time and having the payables department delay payment to the extent possible before the supplier threatens to, or actually does, stop shipment. This type of policy creates significant discontent in your payables department and with suppliers. I know a major company that routinely uses excuses to not pay supplier invoices on time. Consequently, the suppliers dislike dealing with the customer. At some future time the customer will need the suppliers, and the supplier may make it difficult for the customer to obtain the necessary credit and/or favorable credit terms.

Work with key suppliers to define all terms and conditions

Developing an accounts payable strategy can be part of the inventory management program. As discussed in the inventory chapter, the best approach is to work with key suppliers to develop a set of optimal conditions, including quantity, quality, delivery timing, price, credit terms, method of payment, invoicing requirements and the dispute resolute process. I advocate a purchasing management program with accounts payable management a part of the overall supplier relationship. This is a more holistic way of working with key suppliers. The approach is similar to the one you should take with your customers. If you work to establish a true relationship with the supplier, which includes sharing demand information, working together to solve issues and developing new products, you can forge a long-term relationship that will transcend the traditional price negotiations. Having a realistic workable model is important. You need to be able to communicate your vision of a supplier relationship to your key suppliers. Some suppliers will not want to work with you on this basis. It is important to find out early in the process which suppliers are going to be your true supplier partners and focus your purchasing energies on these companies.

Action steps to manage payables

- Form a leadership team.
- Analyze accounts payable.
- Develop a list of current supplier credit terms.
- Establish purchasing standards.
- Define acceptable standard supplier terms and conditions.
- Define performance measures and targets.
- Develop a certified supplier program.
- Develop a strategy for the top suppliers.
- Renegotiate longer credit terms with key suppliers.
- Automate the payment process.

- Review the payables master file.
- Develop payables processing procedures.
- Develop a communications program.
- Develop a training program for accounts payable processing.

These steps comprise an ideal list of actions to take to improve the management of accounts payable. The key is to work on payables management at the same time you are working on inventory reduction. You do not want to have different segments of the organization communicating with suppliers. Changes from the inventory and the accounts payable teams need to be coordinated before they are discussed with the suppliers. Ideally, you want to go to your key suppliers with the new program and get their feedback. They will want to know what it will do for them. Sharing demand forecasts with suppliers and working with them on production scheduling should be a huge benefit to them. This will allow them to better plan their production and reduce costs. You need to share in the lower costs. All suppliers want better pricing, increased sales and faster payment. Determine what is important to the supplier and find a way to satisfy his needs while meeting yours. By developing a full relationship that covers all aspects of the business, you can include longer terms as part of the total package. There will be trade-offs, perhaps, but you can manage them. The key is to have a set of objectives for each major supplier.

Form a leadership team

The leader should be the person responsible for purchasing. You will need a strong leader who is change-oriented. The purchasing manger is the ideal person to lead the accounts payable team since the changes revolve around purchasing and supplier relations. However, if the purchasing manger is not a change agent, you cannot have that person lead the process. I suggest you find a purchasing manger with the skills necessary to carry out the changes recommended. Other members of the team should come from finance, operations and logistics. The finance person should be familiar with accounts payable and payment practices. In larger companies, you will want finance represented by both the treasury and the controllers departments. The personnel from operations and logistics also have a major role in defining materials receiving requirements. This can range from delivery directly to the shop floor, and pallet layout to the type of packaging materials. The details in vendor specifications are very important and will require close communication between customer and supplier.

Analyze accounts payable

Review payments over the past year and determine the top twenty vendors. These vendors should represent 80% to 90% of your purchases. Review a list of suppliers arrayed in descending order by value of purchases. You should have already done this as part of the inventory management program. I am certain you will find that the top twenty vendors supply 80% to 90% of your materials. My experience has been that 5 to 10 of the suppliers account for 80% to 90% of the materials. Determine the average days it takes to pay each supplier compared to the credit terms offered and include this information in your supplier analysis list. Analyze the disputed invoices in your review to determine the reasons for the dispute. Work with suppliers to fix the root causes of the disputes. Meet with suppliers and determine how to resolve the issues. Also, as part of the analysis of accounts payable, review the accounts payable process map made in the value chain analysis. This will help you determine where to reduce time and errors and eliminate defects in processing accounts payable.

List all current supplier credit terms

You will be amazed by the wide variety of credit terms offered. Determine the longest terms offered in your industry and use those as the standard. Compare supplier terms offered by your top twenty suppliers with those currently offered to your top twenty customers.

Establish purchasing standards

Analyze each key supplier's credit-worthiness as you would a top customer. Ask your main suppliers for financial statements. You don't want to work with suppliers who are not financially strong and will not be able to meet your materials requirements. Have your team meet with your key suppliers and review your standards. It is important to understand what they want from the relationship as well as their policies and procedures for doing business. As previously discussed, the agreement with suppliers should cover quantity, quality, price, delivery reliability, invoicing, payment and invoicing method, the dispute resolution process and credit terms. Both product and shipping and packaging standards need to be set for each purchased product. Packaging requirements can even include pallet layout and unit of measure definition. Logistics and materials management personnel need to define material receiving specifications for all raw materials.

Establish standard supplier terms and conditions

These need to be communicated to all suppliers and printed on the purchase order. Use the standard terms and conditions you have established for your invoicing. Your legal counsel must be in charge of writing and enforcing the standard terms and conditions for vendors.

Define performance measures

An early task of the team will be to define accounts payable performance measures. In addition to days of payables outstanding, you will need supplier performance measures. Examine the performance measures your customers are requiring you to meet. That should give you some ideas of what to demand from your suppliers. I suggest that you have the following measures:

- **Days payable outstanding**
  Set tough targets for accounts payable in total and for each key supplier.

- **Delivery reliability**
  Measure how reliable the supplier is in meeting delivery dates and times.

- **Order-to-delivery time**
  Measure the time from order entry to delivery.

- **Product defects**
  Measure product defects per 100,000 units delivered against a standard.

- **Shipping defects**
  Measure shipping defects and/or damage per 100,000 shipments.

- **Invoice presentment time**
  Measure the time it takes to deliver an invoice compared to the ship date.

- **Billing errors**
  Define the maximum number of incorrect invoice lines allowed per 100,000 invoice lines.

- **Time it takes to correct an invoice error or product problem**
  Define the maximum time to correct invoicing and product mistakes and defects. Avoid long-term invoicing and product disputes.

Defining these measures takes time and effort. Meet with key suppliers to work through the measures. Set targets for all measures. You may want to customize the measures for different suppliers. Don't talk about DPO measurers with suppliers. Periodically report on all measures internally and then meet with suppliers to show them the data excluding the DPO information. Discuss how to improve supplier performance against all targets, including price, credit terms and delivery reliability. It is important that good record-keeping systems are developed to track performance against the performance measures.

Develop a certified supplier program

Use the purchasing and payables standards to outline a certified supplier program. Once this program is in place, you will not have to inspect materials on receipt and they can be moved directly to the shop floor, saving you significant time and space. While this activity needs to be a purchasing initiative, it can significantly enhance the inventory and payables management program. With a certified supplier program you can expect on-time delivery of a defect-free product exactly when you need it with correct packaging and error-free electronic invoicing. The inventory and cost reduction from eliminating errors in a certified vendor program is significant.

Develop a strategy for each key supplier

The performance data, along with sharing demand data, working on new products, quantity, quality, and price and credit terms form the basis for vendor negotiations. Even with a certified supplier program you will need to negotiate the specific requirements for each supplier. You can manage trade-offs on all of these issues. Discuss credit terms during these negotiations. Bundle credit terms with other aspects of the contract. These terms must be part of the overall negotiations. Have a strategy for each material and supplier. This will be a critical part of the purchasing and inventory management programs. Accounts payable and inventory management are very closely linked to purchasing. In order to develop the supplier strategy you need to understand what drives the supplier decision-making process and how the sales people are compensated.

Renegotiate credit terms with key suppliers

Once standards are established, start to negotiate longer supplier credit terms. This may require a financial incentive. Do not accept uneconomical incentives. If necessary, offer an incentive in conjunction with another program such as on-time delivery performance.

Automate the payment process

As discussed in the cash management chapter, several steps must be taken to improve payment processing:

- **Be invoiced electronically by key suppliers**
  There are many off-the-shelf e-mail invoicing programs available. Electronic communication will reduce errors and time to process invoices.

- **Pay all major vendors electronically and include the invoice number.**
  This is critical. Don't send checks, which are expensive to process and manage. Every payables system and major bank has the capability to make electronic payments. With electronic check clearing, bank float is virtually eliminated. You must get beyond making payments with checks.

- **Establish a purchasing card system for small value purchases**
  Use the p-card system to assist in managing your purchasing program. Purchasing card companies will help you design purchasing control programs and will supply the data electronically to charge the appropriate expense records. The p-card program will virtually eliminate accounts payable processing. My experience has been that 90% of all invoices account for only 10% of the value of purchases. Eliminate the invoice processing and three-way match for small value purchases. Manage spending control using a p-card, or, if necessary, one of the spend-control systems. The accounts payable department can be reoriented to spot-check payments to key suppliers. Use of the purchasing card will significantly reduce the volume of payments through the bank account, improve purchasing controls, provide supplier-negotiating data and reduce accounts payable processing effort. Internal audit may have more work but if the program is appropriately designed and managed, total payables work and auditing should decline significantly.

Review and refresh the payables master file

This is similar to reviewing the customer master file. Make sure that all the data in the file is correct. Eliminate inactive suppliers. Establish a review cycle that allows a continuous updating similar to a cycle count inventory system. Have the correct name, ship-to and billing addresses, sales contact name, FAX number, e-mail address, phone number, credit terms and any other appropriate data in the master file.

Develop payables processing procedures

- **Make sure no invoice is paid before it is due**
  This merits repeating. I have seen payables departments process invoices early, choosing to pay multiple supplier invoices, some of which are not due, at one time with a single check. While this approach may appear to save work in the payables department, it is not cost-effective. With today's automation, early payment of an invoice never has to be made. Even without automation, you should not pay invoices early. This must become a basic rule in your business.

- **Test supplier late payment grace perio**d
  Every supplier has a late payment grace period it allows before following up on payments. Know what that grace period is for every major supplier. Add it to the credit terms when coding the electronic payment file for each invoice. It will range from one to ten days. Do not go beyond the grace period unless you have previously told the suppler salesperson and payables department what you plan to do and why you need to do so. For example, a cash-flow issue with a major customer may create a payment delay. If you negotiate favorable terms, honor those terms in order to maintain a close relationship with the vendor.

- **Do not take uneconomic discounts to increase net income**
  In general, discounts for early payment are significantly less than your cost of capital. I have seen uneconomic discounts taken in

large companies when divisions were under heavy pressure to meet short-term net income targets. In many instances the EVA and ROTC targets were forgotten in the short run. Don't do it. Develop a chart for the payables department to use in determining whether or not to accept a discount and pay early. Do not take the discount and pay late. You will create huge supplier ill will if you deduct the discount and then pay late.

- **Do not pay the invoice if it is disputed for any reason**
  Your customers don't pay if the invoice is in dispute. You shouldn't do so either unless it is a part of the negotiated certified supplier program with a separate dispute resolution process.

The main point is that payables can be managed in a way that creates significant value for you while maintaining supplier loyalty. You need outstanding suppliers to achieve the inventory levels that are required for excellent customer service.

Develop a communications program

Have a package to send to suppliers that outlines your purchasing program, including method of payment, standard terms and conditions and the information you require to be printed on the invoice. A visit by your finance team member to key suppliers to discuss invoicing and payment may be required.

Develop a training program

Your accounts payable processing department will need to be trained to implement the new policies and procedures. Part of the training should focus on the correct response to collection calls. If the suppler becomes irate, offer to pay immediately with a purchasing card. If the supplier balks at a purchasing card, offer an electronic payment direct to the supplier's bank account.

Summary

You don't have to work on all fourteen recommended actions at once. From discussions with suppliers and a review of disputed invoices, you can determine the most pressing issues and begin to work on them. Accounts payable management can be a key part of your manufacturing excellence program. It is closely linked to the purchasing and inventory management programs. Many of the action steps listed are purchasing issues. By carefully managing the accounts payable and purchasing activities you will ensure a smooth flow of high quality materials, on time at a fair price with maximum credit terms. This will help improve customer service.

Chapter 15

ACCRUED PAYROLL AND EMPLOYEE BENEFITS

Accrued payroll and employee benefits are major current liabilities that must be managed. In my study, accrued payroll and employee benefits average 3.3% of sales and ranged from .1% to 7.7%. The large range was probably due to timing of the payroll payment. A team composed of personnel from the manufacturing, finance, human resources and legal departments should be formed to review payroll and benefits processing.

Outsource payroll processing to a third party. Negotiate the timing for transferring funds to the payroll processor's bank to fund the payroll. I recommend that you transfer funds the same day the payroll is disbursed. If the payroll processing company needs assurance that you will pay, offer a bank guarantee. Have the payroll processing company use your bank for disbursement to avoid issues over the timing of the deposit of funds. You need to make sure you have e-mail notification of payment to all employees. Any change in payroll processing procedures has to be carefully managed by human resources and your lawyers. Many employees do not want electronic payment direct to a bank account. If employees do not have bank accounts, use pre-funded ATM cards. If possible, make this a condition of employment. However, in some states you cannot force employees to accept a direct payroll deposit after they are hired.

Pay employees a maximum of twice monthly. On average, each employee will then have at least one week of accrued payroll. If possible, payment should be made one week after the pay period ends. This provides two weeks of accrued payroll at all times. This payment method should be a condition of employment. For example, if payroll is disbursed on the

15th and the last day of the month, a new employee starting work on the 16th of the month would be paid for work from the 16th through the 23rd for the payroll disbursed on the 31st. The human resources department and lawyers need to verify what payment program can be implemented under state law.

Only pay retirement benefits and administrative service providers when required. Examine payment timing required to meet tax and trust agreements. Do not pay early. The same is true for medical and dental benefits. Only pay when contractually required to make the payment. All of these payments can be managed.

The leadership team can have a direct impact on employee pay practices. The team needs to be involved in all key decisions involving payment frequency and method. Do not leave decision-making solely to the human resources department. Keep in mind that all stakeholders, including employees, need to have an investment in the business.

Chapter 16

EXECUTIVE SUMMARY
Mining the Ca$h Hidden in Your Business

The title of this book, *Mining the Ca$h Hidden in Your Business*, may at first seem rather bold. However, the concepts outlined in the book offer a significant opportunity to free cash locked in your business resulting from inefficient, slow, defective, and non-value-added processes. Determining how to rescue the cash and make it available to fund growth or improvements in your business is the purpose of this book. Once you unlock hidden cash you may even decide to pay bonuses to your employees for meeting working capital targets and pay some of the cash to your shareholders in dividends and/or through share buy-backs.

The following is a summary of the steps to minimize working capital and increase cash flow and reduce financing requirements. It will give you a good overview of how to begin a program to drive down working capital. You will need to read the entire book to fully appreciate and understand what is necessary to manage each component of operating working capital.

You can successfully minimize working capital and in some cases have zero working capital. Current assets can be equal to non-interest-bearing current liabilities. Reducing working capital is a strategic business imperative. It is difficult to grow a company if you have to finance significant increases in working capital. In my study of fifteen manufacturing companies, the average operating working capital was 22.5% of sales and 28.7% of total capital. Thus, working capital is an important investment in a business. Minimizing the investment in working capital will reduce invested capital, improve cash flow and reduce financing requirements. Reducing working capital requires operational excellence and outstanding execution of business processes. You can have the best strategy and product but without excellent processes that allow on-time delivery of defect-free products that meet customer requirements, you will not be successful in the long run. Additionally, without excellent operational and administrative processes, cash flow may be insufficient to grow or even sustain the business.

My definition of working capital is operational in nature. It includes all current assets except strategic cash and current deferred taxes receivable, less all non- interest-bearing current liabilities except other accrued liabilities and current taxes payable and current deferred taxes payable. Short-term debt is excluded from the definition of operational working capital. How you finance working capital is irrelevant to how it is managed. Working capital can be financed with equity, long-term debt, short-term debt or a combination of some or all of them. Strategic cash is all cash not required to operate the business on a daily basis. You need to have a well-designed management program for strategic cash. Excess cash should not be used as a crutch for poor operating execution.

There are some basic points to keep in mind as you begin the process of driving down working capital and significantly increasing cash flow:

- Take time, defects, non-value-added work and variation out of all processes.
- Maintain zero operating cash but have credit lines available to manage cash flow variation and strategic cash reserves for major identified potential risks and investment opportunities.
- Make it very easy for customers to pay quickly.
- Have key materials delivered frequently to meet production requirements.
- Manufacture and ship what you sell as expeditiously as possible.
- Pay invoices only when the supplier expects payment.
- Require all stakeholders to have a financial investment in the business.

The key to reducing working capital and increasing cash flow is to have error-free, fast and flexible operating processes. All processes, from taking an order to receiving payment, must be efficient, error-free and add value.

Reducing working capital is extremely important. As stated above, in my review of fifteen manufacturing companies, operating working capital as a percentage of sales averaged 22.5%. This means that for every $1 million of sales the companies, on average, have invested $225,000 in working capital. A major reduction in working capital significantly increases cash flow and reduces the investment required to grow a business. In my experience, improved inventory turnover and modest reductions in accounts receivable collection time can result in working capital reductions of up to 50% or greater.

Companies with low working capital have a strategic competitive advantage over those with higher working capital requirements. A company with low working capital requirements will have greater cash flow available to invest in the business than competitors with higher working capital needs. The company with lower working capital can be more aggressive on spending to improve the business in areas such as customer service, marketing and product development.

Getting started

Getting started on a working capital reduction program requires some preparation. The following are the key steps to take before taking action on driving down working capital:

- Establish an organization structure. The CEO or COO should lead a team to manage the process. Reducing working capital is a strategic business issue and should not be left to finance to manage.
- Define operating working capital for your company.
- Analyze financial and operating working capital performance for the last twenty quarters.
- Design and install financial and operating working capital performance measures and targets and make them part of the compensation program.
- Analyze the value chain from order-to-cash receipt and determine where you can take time, defects, non-value-added work and variation out of the processes.

At the completion of these steps you will be ready to take action to improve the individual components of working capital. Take the time at the beginning of the program to accomplish these steps. This is analogous to preparing a surface before painting. If you don't do the proper preparation, the paint will not adhere. The same is true of any business improvement project. Without the proper up-front investment of time, energy and money, the full potential of the project will not be realized.

Organization

You will need a strong organization to guide the working capital reduction process. The steps to take in developing an organization are:

- Pick a strong and committed leader.
- Select a solid steering committee team.
- Establish a separate space to hold meetings, information and analysts, if any, working full-time on the project.
- Develop a communications program.
- Establish a training program.

The leader should be the CEO or COO and must be able to communicate the vision of the program. He/she must make sure the changes required to reduce working capital are properly resourced with people and money. The CFO should not be put in charge of the program. Although the finance department has a major role to play in reporting as well as controlling and managing aspects of the program, reducing working capital is not strictly a finance activity.

Working capital definition

It is important that the team agree completely on the definition of working capital. My definition of operating working capital is current assets, excluding strategic cash and current deferred taxes receivable, less non-interest-bearing liabilities excluding accrued liabilities and current taxes payable and current deferred taxes payable. Short-term debt should also be excluded from the definition of operating working capital. It is irrelevant how working capital is financed.

Performance measures

Developing appropriate financial, operating and working capital performance measures is crucial to the success of any working capital reduction program. If you don't measure performance against targets, no improvement will take place. What is measured gets managed and fixed. Make sure your accounting and reporting systems can deliver this information on a routine basis. The key measures must be reviewed. It is important to understand the trends, particularly any changes in trends, in these measurements. It is also necessary to understand why certain levels are achieved and what can be done to improve them. To be successful, the performances measures and targets must be included in the compensation program. If you pay for performance you will get the attention of the workforce.

The working capital performance measures are:

- Operating working capital and each component as a percentage of sales
- Day's sales outstanding in accounts receivable (DSO)
- Inventory turnover
- Days payable outstanding (DPO)

The primary financial performance measures are:

- Sales
- Gross margin
- Earnings before interest and taxes (EBIT)
- Operating margin
- Net income
- Return on sales (ROS)
- Return on equity (ROE)
- Return on total capital (ROTC)
- Total debt to total capital
- Interest coverage
- Operating cash flow
- Operating cash flow as a percentage of total debt

Operational performance measures also need to be computed such as:

- Delivery promises met
- Order-to-delivery time
- Shipping errors per 100,000 shipments
- Product defects per 100,000 units
- Invoicing errors per 100,000 invoice lines

Tailor these measures to meet your specific business requirements. Most importantly, the operational measures should be from the customer's perspective. Meeting your customer's expectations for product quality and delivery reliability is very important.

These measures should be part of your annual operating plan. Report them monthly. Put the results on a bulletin board for all employees to see. Hold monthly meetings to discuss business results and explain your performance against targets and the prior year.

Analyze twenty quarters of past performance to establish a benchmark against which you can compare future performance as process changes are being made. This analysis is very important. It may give you an insight on which component of working capital needs to be addressed first.

Value chain analysis

The value chain is the entire order acquisition-to-cash collection cycle for the company. It includes purchasing and subsequent payment. Map all the processes involved from taking an order to collecting the cash. A good way to get an overview of all the processes is to follow an order from entry to cash collection. The same process can be done for buying parts and raw materials. This analysis will show you where to take time, defects, non-value-added work and variation out of your business processes. This is critical in understanding what steps to take in reducing working capital. The order process must add value to the customer and your business. Your employees should be deeply involved in the order cycle mapping program. They will know the issues in the processes and what needs to be done to fix problem areas. They probably have been waiting for someone to ask them what they would do to improve their processes.

Taking action

Once you are organized, have installed performance measures, analyzed past performance and analyzed the value chain, you are ready to begin a rigorous program of driving down working capital and increasing cash flow. Don't take shortcuts at the beginning. Establishing a baseline against which to measure progress is important. This early work will also tell you where the big successes can be achieved at the beginning of the program. Show strong progress early in the program to increase the enthusiasm of the team. Take the biggest opportunity and put your best people on it.

Current assets

Driving down accounts receivable and inventory is the most important aspect of achieving reduced working capital. Operating current assets are usually significantly greater than non-interest-bearing operating liabilities. Operating current assets are often 30% to 40% of sales. Accounts receivable and inventory are the largest operating current assets. They should be focused on, along with accounts payable, in a coordinated program. Reducing inventory will have a positive impact on accounts receivable and accounts payable management but only if the programs are linked.

To drive down inventory, introduce lean manufacturing techniques. The best place to start in driving down current assets is to examine the disputed item list for accounts receivable and the returns and allowances account. These will tell you the reasons customers are not paying bills on time and returning product. Fixing the root causes of the disputed items and returns will improve customer service, reduce costs and start to drive down working capital.

Managing accounts receivable is the most difficult part of working capital management. No one wants to ask for on-time payments. You can achieve on-time payment of invoices and improved customer service by eliminating administrative errors, shipping errors and product defects. This will also significantly increase customer satisfaction.

Work on reducing operating cash, accounts receivable and inventory while increasing accounts payable at the same time. However, it is important to not have too many programs underway at once. You do not want to dilute your efforts. Focus on the biggest issues and fix them before moving to the next project.

Cash Management

You can operate a business with minimal cash. Operating cash should not be greater than 2% of annual sales. In most cases, you should be able to operate a business with less than 1% of annual sales in cash. You will, however, need to have bank credit lines to manage monthly variations in cash flow. This may not be possible in some instances but you still need to take the steps I recommend to manage your cash. You need to manage cash each day but you do not need large amounts of cash to operate the business on a daily basis. You may need a large amount of strategic cash to protect yourself from a highly volatile business environment but the strategic cash should be separated from operational cash and managed separately.

In many companies, operating cash is 5% or more of sales. Driving cash to below 1% of sales reduces working capital and has a positive impact on return on investment and cash flow. A cash level of 1% is not magic but it is, on average, about one-half week of sales.

Unfortunately, cash is usually excluded from most working capital management programs. It is assumed to be separate from operations and a treasury matter. Cash levels are greatly affected by how invoices are collected and bills are paid. Operations can have a significant influence on operating cash levels. Therefore, operating cash must be included in any operating invested capital performance measurement base.

Steps to take to establish a cash reduction program:

- Select a program leader from the finance team.
- Establish a cash management policy and procedure manual. Ensure separation of duties so no one person manages deposits, bank account transactions and bank account reconciliation. This reduces the risk of fraud and theft.
- Meet with your lead bank to obtain its assistance in designing the program. Establish a bank credit line sufficient to maintain the company in a borrowing position. You may want to change banks if your bank is not helpful.
- Monitor and manage cash balances every day. Borrow cash to meet net needs or use excess cash to pay down short-term debt. Be a short-term borrower at all times.
- List all bank accounts and then close all non-essential accounts.
- Deposit all receipts in one account and make disbursements from a separate account. This will help maintain separation of duties and make it easier to reconcile the accounts.
- List all petty cash accounts and eliminate them. Use purchasing cards instead of petty cash to meet small purchase needs.
- Use purchasing cards for small-value purchases.
- Accept purchasing cards for small-value sales.

These steps are not difficult to accomplish but they will take time to complete. Closing all plant bank accounts and petty cash accounts will be difficult to accomplish. Do not give in to pressure from the plant and administrative staff to retain them. These accounts are costly to manage. Disbursements can be paid and managed with purchasing and travel cards. You need to separate cash management duties, even in the smallest office. Do not allow the same person to deposit receipts and write checks. Cash management is the one area where fraud most often occurs. The nicest, most capable person in finance can turn out to be the biggest thief if lax controls are in place.

Accounts receivable management

The objective of accounts receivable management should be to make it easy for customers to pay quickly. Accounts receivable reduction is the hardest part of working capital management. No one wants to tell the customer he has to pay on time or, better yet, faster. The key to faster collecting is to take time, defects, non-value-added work and variation out of the processes from order entry to collection. You need to remove all the obstacles that delay quick payment. If you ship the correct, defect-free product when requested and send a timely and correct invoice, the customer has no valid reason to not pay on time.

The golden rule of accounts receivable management is to never grant extended credit terms to a customer, even on a temporary basis. The extended terms will become standard. In lieu of extended terms, grant a temporary discount to be paid directly to the customer as a bonus. Do not allow the customer to deduct the discount when paying an invoice because the discount will also become standard even if the payment is late.

Actions to take in minimizing accounts receivable:

- Establish a leadership team.
- Set performance measures and targets.
- Change the name of the credit and collections department to the customer financial services department.
- Perform an analysis of the current state of accounts receivable:

  Age accounts receivable and list them in descending order by size to determine the largest accounts.

  List all credit terms and determine if you can move all customers to the shortest terms.

  List all disputes by type and amount over the last twelve months and start a program to eliminate the causes of the disputes.

  Review the invoice information and layout. Design a better invoice if necessary to make it easy to pay quickly and on time.

- Have correct customer data in the customer master file.
- Involve the sales force in the program.
- Focus on the top twenty customers.
- Negotiate short credit terms in conjunction with improved service programs or, if absolutely necessary, grant economic discounts.
- Settle customer disputes and claims quickly.
- Set fair credit and collection rules and follow them.
- Automate the collection process to the extent possible using electronic payment for large customers and purchasing cards for small-value transactions.
- Establish a rigorous training program for sales and customer financial services.

Focus on the top twenty accounts

Get demand data from your top twenty accounts to better plan production and manage inventory. Visit key customers and determine how you can improve in all areas of the relationship, including administratively. The ideal relationship is to have certified shipments paid on receipt by the customer. This is achievable. Develop a holistic relationship with the customer and involve sales, marketing, logistics and finance personnel when designing packages that provide trade-offs for fast payment. This should be part of a strategic account management program. Offering discounts for faster payment can be linked with sales increases and logistics program improvements. Discounts can be paid at the end of the year as a year-end bonus for paying all invoices on time. This prevents the customer from taking the discount and paying late.

Granting discounts reduces operating income. Even though cash flow is increased, the income reduction is an issue that must be managed. Fewer write-offs for disputed items and lower collection costs can reduce or eliminate the cost of the discount. Discounts can create economic value if the reduction in receivables is large enough to offset the cost of the discount.

Inventory

Inventory management is the heart of any working capital reduction program. You must have operational excellence to achieve significant inventory reduction. The objective is to manufacture only what you sell every day. This is achievable in many instances.

Inventory items can become:

- Obsolete
- Soiled
- Damaged
- Lost
- Stolen

If any of the above occur, you will need to make a charge against income.

Storing inventory also creates expenses for:

- Insurance
- People to move, count and safeguard inventory
- Warehouse space and utilities
- Financing

The best way to reduce the cost is to reduce inventory balances.

The following steps should be taken to begin an inventory reduction program:

- Appoint a leader and leadership team.
- Develop a communication and training program. The changes in manufacturing will be significant and training will be needed to help workers acquire new skills.
- Tour the facilities and improve facility housekeeping and appearance, including enhanced lighting, fresh paint and improved floor coating.

- Review workplace injuries and install safety improvement programs to drive reported injuries to less than 1.
- Review the disputed item list and returns and allowances. Determine what is causing the issues and begin to fix them.
- Review the order-to-shipment cycle to determine process variation and defects. Fix the key production bottlenecks and defective processes. Begin a manufacturing excellence program to reduce production time and increase flexibility while reducing product defects.
- Define operating performance measures.
- Analyze inventory turnover by type of inventory and value to determine the biggest opportunities for reduction.
- Analyze purchases and suppliers of the top twenty raw materials by value. Establish a certified delivery program for key raw materials. Begin to have key raw materials and parts delivered frequently to the factory floor where they will be processed in production.
- Analyze the sales of the top twenty products to determine sales patterns and raw material needs. Determine how to expeditiously manufacture and ship what you sell to large customers. Begin to obtain inventory and projected demand data from the top twenty customers, or those customers generating 80% of sales.
- Analyze product design for simplification opportunities.

Improving manufacturing should be the central part of the working capital reduction program. Achieving manufacturing excellence is key to reducing inventory and accounts receivable. Manufacturing defect-free products when needed and shipping them on time with a correct invoice will increase customer satisfaction and allow you to reduce working capital and increase cash flow.

Other current assets

Other current assets include other receivables and prepaid expenses. These accounts usually range from 2% to 4% of sales. Assign someone to manage other receivables and prepaid expenses. The reason for every item in each account needs to be challenged. Eliminate the need for other receivables and prepaid expenses by providing bank guarantees. Do not make loans to customers or suppliers. If pressed, make a cash payment to help offset customer financing costs.

Current liabilities

Non-interest-bearing current liabilities usually vary between 10% to 15% of sales. Current liabilities can be managed. Managing current liabilities is often done simply by not paying bills on time. In the short run this will work but this approach will not maximize any of the liabilities and, in the case of payroll, it is illegal. It will also result in very poor vendor relations. For a variety of reasons, many companies pay suppliers too quickly or, conversely, far too late. The key is to determine the absolute latest you can pay a bill and then make sure supplier invoices are paid at that time.

Accounts payable

The accounts payable management objective is to pay suppliers when they require payment. You should negotiate economic extended credit terms. Try to trade off increased purchasing and other items of interest to the supplier such as sharing demand forecasts and quick shipment of product for extended terms. When all else fails, offer to pay for extended terms. You only get longer credit terms if you ask for them.

Steps to take in developing an accounts payable management program:

- Form a leadership team.
- Define performance measures and targets.
- Analyze accounts payable to determine payment terms and average time to pay. Begin a program to move all suppliers to the longest terms you are receiving.
- Develop a strategy for the top twenty suppliers and begin negotiating quantity, delivery reliability, quality, price and credit terms at the same time. You need to negotiate a package deal and know what you are willing to trade off for the best overall result.
- Establish purchasing standards.

- Automate the payment process, paying all large suppliers electronically and all small vendors with a purchasing card.
- Establish accounts payable procedures.
- Define acceptable supplier terms and conditions and print them on every purchase order.
- Develop a communication and training program.

Improving accounts payable should be linked with the inventory improvement program to make sure all the steps are coordinated. You need to present one face to the supplier.

Accrued payroll and employees benefits

Accrued employee expenses are a major current liability and must be managed. The key is to challenge how employees are paid. Pay electronically by direct deposit a maximum of twice a month. All stakeholders, including employees, must have an investment in the company. Make sure you are not paying retirement plans or health care providers early. Proceed carefully when making changes in payroll periods. One approach is to make the changes effective only for new hires. Be sure to consult an employment attorney before making any changes to your payment practices. Labor laws in many states are very strict about how employees are paid.

Conclusion

This action program works if you are willing to put it into practice. Make sure your focus is on cash, accounts receivable, inventory and accounts payable. These areas are all linked through operations.

If time is of the essence, I recommend following these fifteen steps to drive down working capital:

- Select a leader and form a leadership team.
- Develop a communications and training program.
- Install working capital performance measures and targets and include them in the compensation package.

- Analyze the value chain and look for opportunities to eliminate time, defects, non-value-added work and variation in the processes.
- Review the disputed item list and returns and allowances and begin to fix the root causes of customer disputes and claims.
- Tour the facilities and establish a program to upgrade them, focusing initially on improving safety, housekeeping, layout, material flow, lighting and facility and equipment maintenance. Make sure you have updated and clean canteen, locker room and restroom facilities.
- Install a safety program to reduce the injury rate to less than one.
- Begin a manufacturing excellence program focusing on defect-free, efficient and flexible manufacturing.
- Redesign the invoice, if necessary, to make it more user-friendly.
- Focus on the top twenty customers:
    - Renegotiate reduced credit terms in conjunction with improved service programs.
    - Develop certified shipment programs.
    - Obtain demand data and use it to forecast production and inventory requirements.
- Set fair and reasonable collection policies and follow them.
- Review and refresh the customer master file.
- Install a daily cash management program.
- Focus on the top twenty suppliers:
- Give key suppliers demand forecasts.
- Renegotiate longer terms in conjunction with purchasing programs.
- Develop a certified supplier program and begin frequent receipt of key materials directly to the shop floor.
- Review and refresh the supplier master file to ensure accurate payment information.
- Automate the collection and payment processes:
- Use electronic receipt and payment for large customers and suppliers.
- Use purchasing cards for small-value sales and small-value purchases. This will reduce accounts receivable and accounts payable transactions and drive down transaction processing costs.

These fifteen steps are critical to driving down working capital, increasing cash flow and reducing financing needs. When they are followed, the result will also be improved customer service and satisfaction, improved employee morale and reduced costs. Customers, employees, suppliers and investors all win with reduced working capital and increased cash flow.

Appendix A

Financial Analysis Example

In this example, I show how to perform the financial analysis recommended in the *Getting Started* section of the book. This can be accomplished using a basic spreadsheet program. The computations can be performed with information from standard financial statements. No adjustments have to be made to the data.

The following is an income statement and balance sheet of a composite manufacturing company based on the averages from my study of fifteen manufacturing companies. The key take-away from this appendix is the actual computation of the performance measures. Also shown is how the returns on capital and cash flow change if you reduce and/or increase each working capital account by 25%.

Balance sheet
($000)

Cash	$20	2.0%*	Short term debt	$25	
			Accounts payable	77	7.7%*
Accts receivable, net	164	16.4%*	Accrued payroll and employee benefits	33	3.3%*
Inventory	125	12.5%*			
Other current assets	26	2.6%*	Other accrued liabilities	50	
Deferred taxes	15		Income taxes payable	15	
Current assets	$350	33.5%**	Current liabilities	$200	11.0%**
Property, plant and equipment	200		Long-term debt	87	
			Other long-term liab.	100	
Other assets	170		Shareholders' equity	333	
Total assets	$720		Total liabilities	$720	

*As a % of annualized sales
**For operating working capital items only

Quarterly income Statement
($000)

		% of sales
Net Sales	$250.0	100.0%
Cost of sales	162.5	65.0
Gross profit	$87.5	35.0
SG&A	62.5	25.0
EBIT	25.0	10.0%
Interest	2.0	
Pre-tax income	23.0	
Income taxes	9.2	
Net income	13.8	5.5%

Working capital management performance measures:

Operating Working capital (OWC) as a % of sales = current assets, excluding strategic cash and current deferred taxes receivable – current liabilities, excluding short-term debt, other accrued liabilities, current taxes payable and current deferred taxes payable / annualized sales

OWC as a % of sales = ($350 - $15 - ($200 - $25 - $65) / 4 x $250) 100% = 22.5%. In this example I have assumed all cash is operating cash.

OWC as a % of sales = ($225 / $1,000) 100% = 22.5%

DSO = accounts receivable / average daily sales

DSO = $164 / ($250 / 91 days) = 59.7 days

Inventory turnover = annualized cost of goods sold / inventory

Inventory turnover = 4 ($162.5) / $125 = 5.2X

DPO = accounts payable / average daily cost of goods sold

DPO = $77 / ($162.5 / 91 days) = 43.1 days

Each working capital account should be analyzed as a percentage of sales as shown above. This analysis provides the relative value of the accounts and, when used with the other working capital measures, allows you to model various actions to reduce working capital.

Financial performance measures:

Gross margin = gross profit / sales = ($87.5 / $250) 100% = 35%

Operating margin = (EBIT / net sales) 100% = ($25 / $250) 100% = 10%

ROS = net income / net sales = ($13.8 / $250) 100% = 5.5%

Interest coverage = EBIT / interest expense = $25 / $2 = 12.5X

Total debt to total capital = total debt / total capital = ($112 / $445) 100%=25.2%

ROE = annualized net income / shareholders equity

ROE = (4 ($13.8) / $333) / 100% = 16.6%

ROTC = (net income + after-tax cost of interest) / total capital x 100%

ROTC =(annualized (net income + (1-tax rate) (interest expense)) / ((short-term Debt + long-term debt) + shareholder's equity) x 100%

ROTC = (4 ($13.8 + .6 x $2) / ($25+ $87+$333)) 100%=13.5%

Operating cash flow (OCF) = net income plus non-cash charges less the change in operating working capital less capital expenditures during the period.

OCF = $13.8 + $11.8 - $11.2 - $25 = -$10.6

In this example, I assumed non-cash charges as a percentage of sales were 4.7% and capital expenditures were 50% of incremental sales, which were the averages from the study. I assumed sales increased 25%, or $50 in the quarter.

Cash flow will be improved with a lower level of working capital. In the example, assuming a 25% improvement in ratios as shown below, operating working capital as a percentage of sales will decline to 12.1% from 22.5%. This is a 46% improvement. If this happens, operating working capital will modestly increase $6 in the quarter and cash flow will only be a negative $5.4, down 49% from a negative $10.6. This will allow the business to grow at 25% with a minimal increase in leverage, over time, to 28.1% from 25.2%. Also, if operating working capital is reduced as shown below, $104 of cash will be generated, which is almost equal to total debt. Assuming the cash is used to pay down debt, total capital will be reduced 23.4% from $445 to $341. If the long-term debt cannot be reduced, then equity should be repurchased. Following my recommended cash management strategy, some short-term debt should be maintained to help maintain zero operating cash.

As discussed, in the above example, working capital can be significantly reduced by achieving a 25% reduction in the ratios.

Action	Impact
Reduce cash to 1.5% of sales from 2%	$ - 5
Reduce DSO to 44.8 from 59.7	- 41
Increase inventory turnover to 6.5 from 5.2	- 25
Reduce other current assets to 2.0% from 2.6%	- 6
Increase DPO to 53.9 from 43.1	- 19
Increase Accrued payroll and benefits to 4.1% from 3.3%	- 8
Total operating working capital reduction	-$104

Improvements of this magnitude are often achievable. Inventory turnover can be improved to at least 8 to 10 turns in most situations. Achieving only half of the target numbers would have a significant impact on cash flow and return on total capital. Perform this type of what if analysis to determine targets for a working capital improvement program.

Appendix B

Weighted Average Cost of Capital

It is important to know your weighted average cost of capital (WACC). In order to create value, longer term, you need to earn a return on total capital above your WACC. Use the WACC to help you make decisions on accepting supplier discounts and granting customer discounts for early payment. Appendix C shows you how to compute economic value added using the WACC compared to the return on total capital of a company.

The weighted average cost of capital (WACC) is the after-tax cost of equity and debt weighted by market value. The components are defined as follows:

- **Risk-free rate** - The ten-year Treasury bond rate
- **Cost of debt** - A company's bond rate, which is the risk-free rate plus a spread. The spread over the risk-free rate varies, depending on a company's credit rating and conditions in the bond market.
- **After-tax cost of debt** - The cost of the company's long-term debt times one minus the tax rate.
- **Cost of equity** - The risk-free rate plus a premium for the risk of equity relative to risk-free debt times the market risk adjustment factor (Beta).
- **Equity risk premium** - The premium that equity commands for the risk of being an equity investor relative to being a debt investor.
- **Total Capital** - Total debt plus equity
- **Equity risk adjustment factor (Beta)** - Beta is a measure of a company's equity risk relative to the total stock market.
  If a company is private it can use the Beta for similar public companies.

An example of the computation of WACC is as follows using the financial statement information from exhibit A:

- Risk-free rate = 5% (long term average ten-year Treasury bond rate)
- Equity risk premium relative to risk-free debt = 5%
- Equity risk adjustment factor (Beta) = 1.2%
- Company cost of debt = 6.5% (risk-free rate plus a spread for corporate debt of 1.5% over 10 year Treasury bonds)
- Equity market capitalization = annual earnings of company x P/E (price to earnings ratio) of the common stock = (4 x $13.8) 15 = $828
- Debt outstanding = $ 112 million
- Tax rate = 40%

This data is very easy to obtain. If you are a private company you can estimate the cost of equity using stock market data for similar types of companies.

You need to know the WACC so you can analyze the economic impact of new investments as well as customer and supplier discounts.

WACC computation:

WACC = (cost of equity x equity weight) + (cost of debt x debt weight)

Cost of equity = (risk-free rate + risk premium) Beta = (5% + 5%) 1.2 = 12%

Equity weight = $828 / ($828 + $112) x 100% = 88.1%

After-tax cost of debt = (5% + 1.5%) (1-.40) = 6.5% x .6 = 3.9%

Debt weight = $112 / ($828 + $112) x 100% = 11.9%

WACC = 12% x .881 + 3.9% x .119 = 10.57% + 0.46% = 11.0%

The important point in the example is that equity is very expensive and is part of the capital invested in the business. Many business people only consider the marginal cost of debt when making working capital investment decisions. This is only true if the investment is temporary. However, as I have discussed, almost all investments in working capital are permanent. Consider the full cost of capital when making working capital decisions. This is no different from analyzing a capital investment project.

Appendix C

Economic Value Added Calculation

The economic-value-added of a firm is important to compute. It is the value being generated above the return expected by investors. EVA can also be negative if a firm is destroying shareholder wealth. EVA is total capital times the return on capital in excess of the cost of capital. The formula for financial value created is as follows:

EVA = (ROTC – WACC) total invested capital

In the example WACC is 11.0% and ROTC in Appendix A is 13.5%. EVA can be computed as follows:

EVA = (return on capital – cost of capital) x total invested capital

EVA = (13.5% - 11.0%) $445

EVA = 2.5% x $445

EVA = $11.1

The company created annualized value of $11.1 above the cost of capital. Over time the rate of change of EVA should be analyzed. The faster EVA grows, the greater the value of the firm. The present value of all future annual EVA approximates the current market value of a company.

In the example in Appendix A, if operating working capital is reduced to $121 from $225, total invested capital declines to $341, assuming the cash generated can be used to pay down debt and/or repurchase shares. In this case, ROTC increases to 17.6%, driving EVA to $22.5, which is a 102% increase in value added.

EVA is a very powerful tool for analyzing the economic impact of various business strategies. It can be used to determine the amount of a discount to offer to a customer to pay quickly and not destroy economic value. It can similarly be used to evaluate whether or not to accept a supplier discount. EVA can also be used to determine the economic implications of increasing or decreasing inventory.

Appendix D

GLOSSARY

The purpose of the glossary is to allow the reader a quick reference without having to refer back to a specific section of the book that includes the definition.

Cash - Includes all cash and cash equivalents such as time deposits and certificates of deposit with maturities of less than one year.

Cash flow - Net income plus non-cash charges and net change in working capital less capital expenditures. This excludes the impact of financing.

Current ratio - Current assets divided by current liabilities. Some credit analysts believe a company has to have a current ratio greater than two-to-one to be considered financially strong.

EBIT - Earnings before interest and taxes. This is sometimes called operating earnings. Examine the income statement to determine how operating earnings are defined for a particular company. Interest expense is sometimes included in operating income.

Economic value added - Economic value added is the return on total capital less the weighted average cost of capital times total capital.

Inventory turnover - Inventory turnover is annualized cost of goods sold divided by inventory on hand. It is a measure of how frequently in a year total inventory is replaced. You should compute it on a FIFO (first in, first out) basis.

Interest coverage - EBIT divided by interest. This shows the amount of pre-tax pre-interest income relative to interest expense. It is a measure of interest coverage or payment risk.

Operating income - Income from operations before special charges, interest and taxes. It is the same as EBIT in many companies. Some companies include interest expense in operating income.

Operating margin - Operating margin is EBIT or operating income divided by net sales.

Days of sales outstanding in accounts receivables (DSO) - Net accounts receivable divided by average daily sales for the sales period. It is a measure of the number of days of sales invested in accounts receivable. DSO should be compared with a company's weighted average credit terms to determine how many days of sales are past due.

Days of payables outstanding (DPO) - Accounts payable divided by the average daily cost of goods sold. DPO is a measure of how many days of cost of goods sold are payable. DPO and DSO should be compared to determine if a company is receiving the same credit from suppliers as is being given to customers.

Net income - Earnings after all expenses, including taxes.

Operating cash flow - Net income plus non-cash charges less changes in operating working capital less capital expenditures during the period.

Operating working capital - Current assets, excluding strategic cash and current deferred taxes receivable, less non-interest-bearing liabilities excluding short-term debt, other current liabilities, current taxes payable and current deferred taxes payable. Strategic cash is excluded since it is not required to operate the business. It should be managed differently from operating cash and shown separately on the balance sheet. Short-term debt is excluded because financing has no impact on the level of operating working capital. You can finance working capital with equity, debt (long and/or short term) or a combination thereof.

Operating working capital as a percentage of sales - Operating working capital, as defined in this book, divided by annualized sales. It is a measure of the percentage of each unit of value of sales invested in working capital.

PE (price to earnings ratio) - The market price of one share of common stock divided by the company's annualized earnings per share.

Quick ratio - Current assets, less inventory, divided by current liabilities. A ratio of one-to-one is thought by some credit analysts to be the minimum for a company to be considered financially strong.

Return on equity (ROE) - Annualized net income divided by shareholders' equity. Many analysts use average equity for the period being analyzed.

Return on sales (ROS) - Net income divided by net sales. It is a measure of profitability.

Return on total capital (ROTC) - Sometimes called return on invested capital or return on total invested capital. ROTC is net income plus after-tax interest expense divided by the sum of total debt plus equity. Some analysts use average capital over the period being analyzed.

Sweep bank account - A bank program that transfers excess cash each day into an interest-bearing account. Cash is swept from the operating account into an interest-bearing account.

Total capital (total invested capital) - The sum of total debt and shareholders' equity. Total capital and total invested capital are used interchangeably.

Total debt - The sum of short-term and long-term debt.

Total debt to total capital - The sum of short-term and long-term debt divided by the sum of total debt and equity.

Weighted average cost of capital (WACC) - The cost of equity times the market value weight of equity plus the after-tax cost of long-term debt times the market weight of debt. This is a measure of the return on capital expected by investors for your company.

Working capital - The traditional accounting definition is all current assets less all current liabilities. In this book I use operating working capital to define the capital employed in operating the business on a daily basis.

Yield - The return on an investment. It is usually used when referring to the return on a debt instrument such as the 90-day Treasury bill yield.

Yield-curve - The curve generated by plotting interest rates for various maturities against time. For example, plotting 90-day Treasury bills, one, two, five and ten year Treasury notes. The slope of the yield curve is carefully watched by an investor as an indicator of the bond market outlook for inflation.